PRE-COLUMBIAN ARCHITECTURE

THE GREAT AGES OF WORLD ARCHITECTURE

BAROQUE AND ROCOCO   *Henry A. Millon*

CHINESE AND INDIAN   *Nelson I. Wu*

EARLY CHRISTIAN AND BYZANTINE   *William L. MacDonald*

GOTHIC   *Robert Branner*

GREEK   *Robert L. Scranton*

JAPANESE   *William Alex*

MEDIEVAL   *Howard Saalman*

MODERN   *Vincent Scully, Jr.*

PRE-COLUMBIAN   *Donald Robertson*

RENAISSANCE   *Bates Lowry*

ROMAN   *Frank E. Brown*

WESTERN ISLAMIC   *John D. Hoag*

PRE-COLUMBIAN ARCHITECTURE

by Donald Robertson

GEORGE BRAZILLER · NEW YORK · 1963

To my dear friend and late colleague,
Alice Parkerson

All rights reserved.
For information address the publisher,
George Braziller, Inc.
215 Park Avenue South
New York 3, New York

Library of Congress Catalog Card Number: 63–7517

Printed in the Netherlands

First Printing

Printed in photogravure and letterpress by Joh. Enschedé en Zonen, Haarlem, The Netherlands. Set in Romulus with Spectrum display, both faces designed by Jan van Krimpen. Format by William and Caroline Harris.

CONTENTS

Text

1 PROLEGOMENON

In November of 1519 Cortés crossed the high eastern passes between snow-capped volcanoes and descended into the central Valley of Mexico, finally reaching Tenochtitlán, capital of Montezuma and principal seat of the Aztecs.[1] His amazement and that of his followers at what they saw is preserved for us in the almost laconic sixteenth-century accounts of that fabulous city. Rising on an island in Lake Texcoco, linked to the mainland by great causeways, Tenochtitlán was dominated by towerlike pyramids crowned with gleaming temples, blackened inside with the smoke of copal incense and reeking with the smell of burning human hearts sacrificed to the hungry gods. Groups of monumental buildings integrated with architectural sculpture and dramatized with fresco paintings rose from plazas connected by streets broad and straight, aqueducts, canals, and bridges. The plazas, which served to punctuate focal points, were part of the regular gridiron plan of the city.[2] In the heart of the capital were palaces surrounding spacious courtyards and carefully cultivated gardens, ball courts, markets, private houses, and the many other elements one finds in a modern metropolis. There was even an aviary and a zoo for wild animals.[3] Indeed, Tenochtitlán was closer to our idea of a well-designed city than any in the Spain of the conquistadors. As Cortés and his men approached the capital, it must have floated before their eyes like an enchantment from *Amadis of Gaul* or some other popular Spanish romance of chivalry.[4] (See plates 13, 14.)

No city in Spain and few anywhere in all Europe could have compared with what the Spaniards actually saw in the orderly pattern of its plan, in its cleanliness, in the wealth it drew from its tributary provinces, or even in the number of its people.[5] During the Conquest of Mexico all was destroyed, all swept away with such thoroughness that now little remains of Tenochtitlán, the site of present-day Mexico City,[6] except some few pieces of architectural sculpture, the lower stages of the main pyramids, and the written accounts of Cortés, Bernal Díaz del Castillo, and the Anonymous Conqueror.[7] Colonial buildings cover the site of the great temple, and the National Palace replaces the Palace of Montezuma (plate 15).

Cortés overthrew the Triple Alliance of the Culhua Mexica, although he is often given credit for destroying the empire of Montezuma.[8] There was no such thing; Montezuma was the ruler of México-Tenochtitlán and head of only one member of a Triple Alliance including Texcoco, the cultural center across the Lake of Texcoco from Montezuma's capital, and Tlacopan, present-day Tacuba, a minor subdivision of Mexico City. The domains of the Triple Alliance included most of central and southern Mexico; they surrounded Tlaxcala, an independent enclave, and bordered the lands of the Tarascans to the west of México-Tenochtitlán.[9] Outside the orbit of the Aztecs and their dominions lay the lands of the Maya to the east in the peninsula of Yucatán extending into present-day Honduras, British Honduras, and Guatemala. The Maya were the makers and bearers of a related but more sophisticated culture in Middle America. Because of the many traits separating them from the peoples to the west, it is more convenient to talk of "Mexican" in contrast to "Maya" civilization.

The civilizations of the Andean region are so distinct from the cultures of central and southern Mexico that we shall find it more meaningful to treat them quite apart from both the Mexican and Maya traditions. One can compare these cultural differences to the linguistic divisions of Europe: the Mexican and Maya are different to the extent that Spanish is different from Italian. Like the Romance languages they are related, and thus make a telling contrast when we compare them to those of the Andean civilizations—a comparison of the order of magnitude of German compared with Italian or Spanish.

The Aztecs shared with most of the people under their power in central and southern Mexico a way of life and a particular kind of civilization that George C. Vaillant has called the "Mixteca-Puebla Culture."[10] The common denominators of this late pre-Conquest period were religion, calendar, and technological and artistic styles which were either identical among these people or minor variations upon fundamentally similar themes. Like all the peoples of Middle America, they had corn as the abiding staple of life; like all agricultural peoples, they had a powerful interest in the forces of nature—rain and sun which could guarantee good crops.

These forces of nature quite naturally appear in the religious aspect of Middle American life.[11] Tlaloc in his several guises presided over rain; tender young corn was personified by

9

Xilónen, and a more general maize or corn god by Cinteotl. Tonatiuh, the Sun, was one of the paramount gods, and worshiped with human sacrifice. Gods were also personifications of human activities. Thus, Tlazoltéotl was goddess of filth and carnal love (a provocative juxtaposition to be sure); Huitzilopochtli (Humming Bird of the Left) was the tribal god of the Aztecs and a powerful war god; Tezcatlipoca, called Smoking Mirror, the god of fortune and chance, was known in several guises—among them the Black Tezcatlipoca of the North. Quetzalcoatl (the White Tezcatlipoca of the East, the Feathered Serpent), was a god of wisdom and learning; he was associated with the planet Venus and also known as Ehécatl, God of the Winds to whom round temples were built.[12] As one of the aspects of Tezcatlipoca, Quetzalcoatl joined Huitzilopochtli, the Blue Tezcatlipoca of the South. The Red Tezcatlipoca of the West was Xipe-Tótec, a vegetation and fertility god. To the Mixteca-Puebla culture, as to classical antiquity in Europe, this complexity and even confusing shifting of attributes was accepted as part of the nature of the divine. Tezcatlipoca with his four colors and four directional associations represented a fourfold division of the universe. Quetzalcoatl and his twin, a hunting god Xolotl, the monster, suggest the cosmos as duality—a duality expressed by Ometecuhtli and his wife Omecihuatl, the first couple, the creator gods.

These two ways of conceiving of the universe are reflected in Aztec architecture. The city plan of México-Tenochtitlán, for instance, is divided into four parts by four avenues meeting in the main plaza, the religious heart of the city (plates 13 and 15). The duality of nature is also reflected in the representative Aztec pyramid on which two temples stand side by side (plate 29). México-Tenochtitlán, one was dedicated to Huitzilopochtli, the war god, the other to Tlaloc, the rain god. They thus represented war, a human activity, and rain, a natural phenomenon, both essential to the survival of the people.

As intermediaries between the people and the all-important gods, the priesthood played a major role in the life of the state. Since religion and secular affairs were not divisible, Montezuma was head of both church and state. The resources of the society in both its aspects were marshaled in support of religious architecture. The temple on its pyramid, even more than the church in the Christian world, was the focus of the architectural activities of the people. Secular buildings were relatively less important and less substantial, for the labor needed to raise the pyramids, prepare their facings, and fit them with religious sculpture and fresco painting placed heavy enough demands upon a people living essentially at the neolithic level. Thus, other types of monumental buildings were few.

Religion included control over time as well as support of the gods. Time was not only the change of the seasons, but it was also the past and the future in a predictable pattern of cyclical duplication. A ritual calendar called Tonalpohualli, "sun calendar," was 260 days long and was complemented by a secular calendar 365 days long, divided into 18 months of 20 days each and 5 intercalated extra or, "dead," days (Nemontemi). At fifty-two-year intervals these two calendars coincided, ending the old and beginning the new together. Each new fifty-two-year cycle was inaugurated with great pomp and religious rites, called the New Fire Ceremony, to celebrate the fact that the world had begun again. The New Fire was kindled by a wooden drill on a fireboard like the one in a detail from the pre-Conquest manuscript Codex Nuttall (plate 1), showing the feathered drill, the board with its holes, and a sign for smoke and flame. To mark the end of the old epoch, pottery was ritually destroyed and fires extinguished to be relit during the New Fire Ceremony. Temples and pyramids were probably rebuilt each fifty-two years to celebrate the cyclical renewal of the world.[13]

The calendar of the Aztecs can be considered a less elaborate form of the Maya one, the complexity of which is unique in the New World. To the Maya, the counting of time and the passage of the years were in themselves priestly and divine activities. In the cosmic order of the universe the gods in sequence picked up the burden of time from their predecessors who relinquished it. Carved stone stele with detailed records of dates marked the passage of time among the Maya (plate 72). Set in large plazas before temples, they were essentially markers of architectural space. So closely did they adhere to their architectural role that they were, in the strict sense of the phrase, architectural sculpture rather than mere sculptural monuments (plate 69).

Despite the common religious and calendrical traits, however, the Mixteca-Puebla culture was not composed of people conforming to a rigid ecumenical system. Regional variations existed, so that the religion of the Aztecs was not completely identical with that of their subject peoples. Painting and sculpture, as well as architecture, show local variations on basic themes from city to city throughout Mexico; regional styles survived throughout this period of cultural unification.

The different emphases given to various aspects within the Mixteca-Puebla culture reflect the local traditions and languages of individual city-states which made up the territories of the Triple Alliance in both central and peripheral Mexico.[14] To a certain extent, architectural styles reflected these linguistic differences. The pyramid and temple of the Aztecs are as different from the Maya versions of this architectural motif as the people and the language are from each other.

The diversity among geographical areas of Middle America permitted a wide range of settings for its architecture. Teotihuacán (plate 36), Cuicuilco, Malinalco, and Mitla are all in valleys of the central plateau, ringed by impressive heights. Chichén Itzá (plate 57) and Uxmal are on the flat, slightly rolling limestone plain of northern Yucatán. Lakes conditioned the settings of both places in the Petén Lake area of southern Yucatán and México-Tenochtitlán in central Mexico (plate 13). El Tajín is in the rolling, heavily forested lands of the east coast, while Monte Albán looks down upon the Valley of Oaxaca from its location on a dominating mesa. Tulum, on a cliff overlooking the Caribbean Sea, is one of the most dramatic northern Yucatán sites (see p. 113).

The differences of climate and geography partially influenced the various architectural styles, and geological differences helped to determine the preferred building materials. Volcanic rock was used in the highlands; one called *tezontli* by the Aztecs is a particularly beautiful porous stone ranging in color from black to a crimson red. The limestone of northern Yucatán was easily worked as masonry and was also adaptable to complex carving. Furthermore, it could be burned to make serviceable plaster and mortar. Tropical hardwoods made almost indestructible lintels which the Maya needed to support the ponderous weight of their masonry vaults. Throughout Mexico rubble fill and adobe, or sun-dried-mud brick, were durable when covered with a waterproof skin of stucco or plaster which was made from burned limestone. However, more monumental stone facings were created from large sculptured plaques or mosaiclike compositions of small, carefully fitted pieces of stone. A wide range of colors used for mural paintings and for polychroming architecture and sculpture came from the resources of the earth, both mineral and vegetable.

Mexican history began with traces of early man, probably dating from the Pleistocene era. Projectile points of human manufacture have been found in conjunction with bones of the extinct mammoth at Ixatapan, and fossil remains were discovered at Tepexpan near Mexico City. A date as early as 12,000 to 8,000 B.C. has been proposed for these beginnings.[15]

A great time gap separates Tepexpan man from the earliest evidences of civilizations high enough to produce monumental architecture. In central Mexico the first major work is the Pyramid of Cuicuilco (plates 8, 9); in the Maya area architecture begins with Pyramid E VII Sub at Uaxactún (plates 92, 93). Both these structures are ascribed by archaeologists to the pre-Classic, or Formative, period, the earliest period found so far with a proper architecture (see chart, page 115).

The Classic period that followed is an archaeological designation representing a period when the various components of Middle American civilization reached peaks of accomplishment. During this period the great site of Teotihuacán (plates 33–42) in the central Valley of Mexico reached the height of its development and was complemented by such sites as El Tajín in Veracruz (plates 10, 11), Monte Albán to the southeast (plates 20–26), and Xochicalco to the south (plate 52). Even as far away as Guatemala, Kaminaljuyú is related by its architecture and pottery styles to Teotihuacán. In the Maya area the Classic period was the time of the great sites of Tikal in the Petén (plates 84–90); Uxmal in northern Yucatán (plates 96–102); Copán to the south (plates 68–72); and Palenque in the Usumacinta River Valley (plates 74–80).

The decline of the high civilizations of the Classic period is marked in central Mexico by the rise of the Toltecs at Tula (plates 43–51) in the post-Classic period. At a later date invaders from the Toltec region moved across the Gulf of Mexico to northern Yucatán and established themselves as conquerors at Chichén Itzá (plates 57–60, 62–67), inaugurating the Mexican period in the history of the Maya. Our knowledge of events in the post-Classic period is more extensive and precise than our knowledge of the Classic. It is based on native chronicles and accounts of the Toltec migrations which survive both in written documents and in native pictorial manuscripts. The architectural similarities between Tula and Chichén Itzá would seem to confirm these native historical accounts.[16]

When the Toltecs invaded Yucatán, they brought the neighboring Maya into the large pattern of conquest and reconquest that dominated central and peripheral Mexico. Until then, the Maya, living behind mountain barriers, isolated by the sea and difficult swampy jungle terrain, were separated from the rest of Mexico, free to work out their own destiny uninterrupted by constant invasions. Their isolation was comparable to that of Egypt, and they were able to develop local architectural styles of a thousand years' duration. Central and peripheral Mexico were more like Mesopotamia, with a history of invasions and new art styles superseding but at the same time being influenced by the old. Architectural development within the Maya region was relatively constant, in contrast with the ruptures separating Cuicuilco from Teotihuacán, Teotihuacán from Tula, and Tula from México-Tenochtitlán in central Mexico or the distinct regional styles of El Tajín, Monte Albán, and Mitla in peripheral Mexico.

The remains of Teotihuacán point to a violent and sudden end to this Classic period city. Tula, too, was taken by force in the middle of the twelfth century, according to native historical traditions and archaeological evidence. The "Burned Palace" (plate 51) was destroyed, and the columns from the Temple of Tlahuizcalpantecuhtli (plates 44, 47–49) were overthrown and buried in pre-Hispanic times. In the fourteenth century, following the destruction of Tula in central Mexico, the Aztecs and other related peoples entered the Valley of Mexico. They adopted the Mixteca-Puebla culture, probably from the Mixtec areas of the present-day states of Puebla and Oaxaca (see Maps A and B, p. 113). Historical manuscripts composed before the Spanish Conquest recount the history of these Mixtec peoples, beginning as far back as the seventh century A.D. (See Codex Nuttall, plate 1.)

Patterns of native history, like patterns of native architecture, help us to understand human behavior in a broad sense, for we consider native America to have developed from its pre-Formative beginnings without any appreciable contact with the Old World. The reasons for studying the architecture of the New World are thus several. Its intrinsic aesthetic worth looms largest, and is the subject of the following pages, but architecture also gives us insight into the religion and the culture of the human societies that created it. The architectural heritage of the Old World is part of our cultural heritage, but that of the New World shows us how the native peoples of America arrived indepen-

14

dently at similar solutions to similar problems. Pre-Columbian architecture, by its distinctness from that of the Old World, proves its isolation, but its solutions to problems which also faced Old World architects suggest constants deriving from architecture as a human activity.

2   MIDDLE AMERICA

The Aztecs thought of their temples as houses of the gods; the Nahuatl word for temple was *teocalli*–literally, divine house. These were monumental structures based on the form of an ordinary native house with a flat roof supported on wooden beams, although sometimes it was covered with a peaked and thatched roof. Codex Mendoza (plate 2) shows both types.[17] The native house was often built upon a low mound or step to raise it above the ground. The pyramid was that mound or step increased in area, height, and mass in order to give importance to the divine house. It is an architectural irony that the pyramid grew in time to almost unbelievable size (the Pyramid of Cholula is larger in area than any of the Egyptian pyramids), while the temple upon it stayed relatively closer in proportion to its prototype, the native house.

When the Aztecs in the sixteenth century called the Pyramid of Cholula *tlachiuhaltepetl*, or artificial hill, they were describing not its function but its form, for it was a man-made mound covered with a "skin" of masonry or plaster. This was not a pyramid in the sense the geometer uses the word nor in terms of the Egyptian pyramid with its funerary function.[18] The Middle American pyramid was, if anything, closer to the ziggurat of Mesopotamia. Both were constructed in several giant stages or horizontal divisions (plates 34, 35, 37, 46, 85–87, 92), sometimes called steps, and both were platforms for supporting temples.

The periodic rebuilding of pyramids was a widespread practice in Middle America, a process of enlarging and rejuvenating religious architecture. When a community wished to enlarge its

15

pyramid, it was customary to destroy the temple on top and cover the existing pyramid with a mass of fill, burying the original facing within the new structure. Then a new facing was put on the enlarged pyramid, and a new temple erected on top, thus preserving an onionskin sequence of forms within a pyramid, the multiple façades of previous building phases preserved under the last. The plans and elevations of Tenayuca (plate 29) show very clearly the laminated nature of that pyramid. At sites such as Cholula, one can enter the mass of the pyramid through tunnels dug in the rubble fill and see the still-preserved original facings of earlier constructions. In some cases the system was slightly varied, so that, as at the Temple of the Warriors, Chichén Itzá (plates 62, 63), the original temple was partly preserved and filled with earth to make a solid foundation for the later pyramid built over it. The Acropolis at Piedras Negras shows the complex result of long periods of construction and rebuilding (plate 81).

The ritual role of the pyramid for the Maya area can be reconstructed from present-day practices at the Indian pueblo of Chichicastenango, Guatemala. In this small market town two churches face each other across the main plaza. Like Maya temples, both are built upon raised platforms which have staircases leading up to the front entrance. The platforms function much the way pyramids functioned in relation to temples—as massive monumental supports. On Sundays the Indians come to Chichicastenango from the surrounding countryside to buy and sell in the market and to perform their religious obligations much as their pagan Maya ancestors did. They make their confessions to native priests and recite pagan prayers in their Indian language. They burn incense at the base of the staircases and on the platforms in front of the buildings as well as inside. Great clouds of smoke fill the interiors and over a long period of time have completely blackened them. Gilded carved-wood baroque altarpieces look like ebony, and paintings have slick bituminous surfaces. Just as the architecture is a blend of pagan and Christian elements, so religion at Chichicastenango is a mixture of Maya survivals with Christian addenda. The burning of *pom*, the pagan Maya incense, outside and inside the building and the recitation of prayers in the Indian language to native priests represent a continuity with times past.

There is no such clear-cut survival of old ways in either the central or peripheral areas of Mexico, but early colonial manu-

16

script paintings document some phases of Aztec religious practices. The Codex Magliabecchiano (plate 4) illustrates human sacrifice taking place on the pyramid platform in front of a temple, with spectators on the ground below. The pyramid is an elevated theatrical stage on which the religious drama is enacted, and the temple proper functions almost like scenery; at the same time it houses the image of the god and paraphernalia of the cult. We know from eyewitness accounts of the conquistadors that the interior was dark from clouds of incense, as in the churches of Chichicastenango, and that it reeked with the smell of blood collected in the *cuauhxicalli*, or Eagle Vase, and burned hearts of human sacrificial victims.[19]

The pyramid also functioned as a military structure, the place of last resort when a town was attacked. Codex Mendoza (plate 2, upper center) shows Moquihuiz, king of Tlatelolco (a division of México-Tenochtitlán at the time of the Conquest), falling from the great pyramid of his city when he was defeated by the Aztecs. Throughout the section of this manuscript recording Aztec conquests, the symbol of a defeated town is a temple, roof askew, with signs for fire and smoke billowing forth.

Remains of the temple proper in central and peripheral Mexico are rare, but from the few examples still extant we learn that it was a simple rectangular building of one and sometimes two rooms, with a flat ceiling supported by wooden beams. There were no windows; the sole source of light was a single door. According to pictorial sources, the Aztec temples had great flying façades, or false fronts, which were probably built of wood, rising above the main façade and carrying special designs indicating the god housed within, all adding to the apparent height and the significance of the temple building (see plate 2, upper center).

The representative Maya temple had a flat roof, and sometimes rising above it, a great roof crest or roof comb (plate 53). Like the decorated *fronton*, or flying façade, of the Aztec temple, the roof comb added to the height and thus to the architectural importance of the building. The flat roof covered vaulted rooms embedded in a great windowless mass of masonry. A single doorway served both as entrance and as the only source of light. The vaults were constructed on the principle of the corbeled arch (plate 54),[20] in which horizontal rows of stones were laid, beginning at the top of opposite side walls. Each row overhung the one below it, like checkers or dominoes piled in step fashion, until two such corbelings reached the center of the room, where they were linked by a series of capstones running the length of the vault. The vault had the appearance of two inclined planes meeting and resting on each other at the highest point of the interior space. Stability was achieved by weighing down the upper surface of the vault with masonry (cement and rubble fill), so that sheer weight kept the individual stones from shifting out of position. Thus they could support their load and at the same time, when the cement set, maintain their form. The vault and fill became to all intents and purposes a single monolith of masonry. The roof comb acted as an added weight, forcing the whole construction into a more solid and stronger unity.

Externally, the Maya temple consisted of two or sometimes three zones (plates 76, 86). The first and lowest was the supporting wall, generally left as a flat unsculptured plane and crowned with a cornice to separate it from the second zone, the level of the vault. The vault zone frequently received a rich decorative treatment of lattice motifs and great mosaic masks. The third zone, when it existed, was the false front, or *fronton*. This, too, was separated from the zone beneath by a cornice, and was in turn decorated with sculpture. In addition, some buildings had the roof comb. The lowest zone, with its simple flat plane, expressed its function as a solid bearing-wall, to support and insure stability. The elaborately rich ornamental sculpture on the second and third zones and the pierced, almost filigree design of the roof comb were all devices for lightening the apparent weight of the ponderous and heavy vaults. The delicate tracery of the roof comb acted as a transition between the solid mass of building and the sky, further lightening the visual effect.

The sequence of pyramids in central Mexico records the architectural history of this area from pre-Classic times to the Spanish Conquest. The Formative Pyramid of Cuicuilco, buried in a lava flow just south of Mexico City (plates 8, 9), was built by an unknown people at an early date, possibly even before the Christian era. It is of a majestic size (over 380 feet in diameter and 65 feet in height) and simplicity of form. This early monument enunciates principles that continued to be of importance in Mexican architecture. The temple, now destroyed, was small and unimportant in comparison with the size of the pyramid, which was built in a series of steps, or stages. The original pyramid was two stages high, but later was rebuilt to four. A staircase extending up the front, across all the various stages, helped to unite them compositionally. The plan, an immense circle, and the location of a ramp on the side opposite the staircase,[21] make this pyramid atypical.

The builders of Teotihuacán also remain unknown to us, because the city was already a ruin when the founders of Texcoco entered the Valley of Mexico. The latter left us, in the Codex Xolotl, one of the best native pictorial sources for the ancient history of the region.[22] Excavations at Teotihuacán have been going on for a hundred years with exciting discoveries still being made.[23]

The Pyramid of Quetzalcoatl in the citadel group at Teotihuacán (plate 38) has a richly sculptured façade which creates patterns of light and shade almost baroque in their intensity—an effect never attained in later times outside the Maya area. It is remarkable that all the stone facing of this building was removed, except from the main façade, which was covered by a later rebuilding (plate 37). The later pyramid built against this ornate and richly carved façade now seems almost puritanical in its insistence upon flat planes and simple frames, although we know that originally architectural painting created coloristic effects which are now lost. Both the early and later pyramids show the characteristic Teotihuacán elevation. On each stage there is a lower sloping surface, or talus, best known by its Spanish name, *talud*, and an overhanging vertical panel with a severe rectilinear frame called the *tablero*. Similar *taluds* and *tableros* are to be seen at the related sites of Cholula, near Puebla, and Kaminaljuyú, near Guatemala City. At Cholula paintings on the *taluds* have been preserved, and at Teotihuacán *tablero* paintings still exist, for example in the "Temple of Agriculture." The two pyramids of the Moon and of the Sun (plates 34 and 35), the latter being the largest at Teotihuacán, presented structural problems in the construction of the *tableros* because of the great height of the individual stages of the pyramids, with the result that *talud-tablero* construction was limited to smaller outbuildings and subordinate platforms.

Tula (plates 43–51), the home of the Toltecs, is the first central Mexican site in a chronological sequence to come down to us with a historical setting. The sources describing the Toltecs and their capital at Tula are impressive in the amount of information they convey.[24] The Temple of Tlahuizcalpantecuhtli[25] is significant because of the new contributions it makes to architectural design. Study of the temple has revealed that the wooden ceiling

19

was originally supported by a row of four telemones depicted as warriors in full caparison and behind them a row of four square stone columns with carving on all four faces (plates 44, 47–49). These columns are composed of separate drums joined with a mortise and tenon joint. The entrance was through an opening three units wide, and the lintel was supported by two feathered serpent columns with heads on the floor and bodies rising to the lintel, similar to those serpent columns found at Chichén Itzá (plate 63).

In its lower stages (plates 45, 46) the pyramid preserves the *tableros* and *taluds* with lighter frames than those at Teotihuacán. Because they are compound, or overlapping on three different planes, they have more interesting planar and spatial relationships. Those establishing the plane of the wall have a monstrous face with a human head in its mouth; those of the next plane show a series of vultures and eagles devouring human hearts; and finally, those projecting most from the wall plane have a frieze of stalking felines. All were originally polychromed.[26]

The characteristic Aztec pyramid (plate 29) discarded the *tablero-talud* relationship for a more simple design in which the faces of each stage of the pyramid sloped as though they were a series of *taluds* with no crowning *tablero*. The wall of the temple, however, still has vestiges of the *tablero-talud* articulation in a characteristic molding, indicating a break in the wall plane. Double staircases rise to twin temples on the single pyramid, and flanking these staircases is a framing unit, breaking at a molding near the top and changing the angle to create a small pedestal flanking the top of each staircase—a pedestal which probably supported a piece of sculpture (plate 30). The well-preserved Pyramid of Teopanzalco at Cuernavaca is a fine example of this style (plate 31), and unusual in that the lower walls of the twin temples are still preserved *in situ*. Tenayuca (plates 27–30) is a well-explored and well-reconstructed Aztec pyramid easily reached from Mexico City.

Literary references and early colonial drawings preserve information about the great Pyramid of México-Tenochtitlán, with its twin temples to Tlaloc and Huitzilopochtli; but little has been discovered in the actual excavation of this most important Aztec pyramid.[27] We are more fortunate, however, in another significant pyramid of this area, where current excavations are bringing to light the great Pyramid of Tlatelolco. Aztec historical sources state that the people of Tlatelolco began to build their pyramid to rival—especially in terms of size—the pyramid of

México-Tenochtitlán. This challenge was considered an affront so gross that the Aztecs of México-Tenochtitlán felt compelled to attack the Tlatelolcans. Defeated, the Tlatelolcans lost their independence, and their city became a part of México-Tenoch-titlán, as it is a part of Mexico City today.

Peripheral Mexico has given us the Classic period sites of El Tajín and Monte Albán and the post-Classic Aztec period sites of Calixtlahuaca and Malinalco. Themes similar to those of central Mexico dominate peripheral Mexico, but at El Tajín and Monte Albán variations on these themes show considerable difference in artistic form. The Aztec period sites, on the other hand, show somewhat less regionalism.

El Tajín (plates 10, 11) and its subdivision, El Tajín Chico, stress an aesthetic of strong contrasts of light and shade. This is especially clear in the Niche Pyramid, with its 364 deep niches which were possibly filled with sculpture of calendrical significance. The upper edge of each stage is crowned by a great projecting molding reminiscent of the cymae of Roman or Florentine Renaissance architecture, creating strong horizontal patterns through the manipulation of light and shade.

Monte Albán (plates 20–26), on the other hand, suggests closer ties with the formal patterns of central Mexico. *Taluds* and *tableros* remind one of the complexities of Tula design rather than the forthright rectilinearity of Teotihuacán. *Tableros* at Monte Albán (plate 22) are made on two overlapping planes and seem to hang where the ends are dropped in step fashion at the corners. They are distinct from the later compound *tableros* of Tula (plate 46), however, because of their lack of relief sculpture. Although the overlapping planes of the Monte Albán *tableros* do not create such great contrasts of light and shade as the moldings and niches of El Tajín, the geometric relationships they establish are certainly more subtle.

Calixtlahuaca is remarkable for its round pyramid (plate 5) and the sculpture of Quetzalcoatl as Ehécatl, God of the Winds, found inside the temple. An altar, in plan suggestive of the Egyptian cross, or ankh, decorated with carved skulls and having a wall of two planes, is prominent among the unusual structures at the site (plates 6, 7). Malinalco (plate 12), in contrast, is remarkable for a number of temples cut from the living rock. Here architecture is truly sculpture; small details such as the front walls of buildings and roofs are added to architectural forms which are essentially sculptural subtractions from the natural matrix of the mountainside. Even here, however, the temple is carved so that it stands upon a platform, and the subordinate sculpture, movable at other sites and thus lost, is part of the monolithic whole. The bench inside the circular temple at Malinalco is carved with the skins of ocelots and eagles in the shape of cushions, and the main entrance is carved into the face of Tepeyollotl, the earth monster.

Maya pyramid design is of such richness and diversity extreme examples can only begin to suggest its scope. The Formative period pyramid of Uaxactún, called prosaically E VII Sub (plates 92, 93), is one of the earliest discovered so far in the Maya area. An uncommon type,[28] it is radially symmetrical in plan. On each of the four sides is a staircase flanked by a series of stuccoed masks representing as many as three building periods. The use of masks and the entrant angles at the four corners of the several stages of the pyramid all function as parts of a close-knit unified whole and establish patterns to be followed later in the Maya area.

As it was excavated with its rebuilding and additions, E VII Sub was one of the most sculptural of all Maya structures. The various stages and the sculptured masks are masterfully integrated into the plastic whole of the architecture. The staircases flow like some slow viscous substance down the four sides of the main mass, divide, and seem to embrace the lower order of masks. Though historically unrelated, this pattern of staircases and masks is strikingly similar to Michelangelo's treatment of the staircase-balustrade relationship in the Laurentian Library in Florence (plate 94). Like Michelangelo, the anonymous architects of E VII Sub created patterns of tension between the central path of the staircase and the flanking variants, willfully interrupting the orderly sequence of the staircase with intrusive elements for aesthetic ends. One is justified in assuming that a building of such architectural subtlety as E VII Sub is the culmination of experience gained from many examples, now lost, in which architectural forms were being defined and refined.

The Maya pyramid type found at Tikal (plates 85–87) is also quite different from the pyramids of central and peripheral Mexico. Despite the greater number of stages, often steeper slant, and resulting greater height—proportional as well as actual—it gives less of an effect of a series of clear-cut horizontal divisions. The stages are closely integrated through the use of a similar sloping angle for both the *talud* and *tablero* elements. This

22

angle sometimes approaches the over-all angle of the slope of the main mass of the pyramid. A series of entrant angles at the corners of the Maya pyramid, sometimes combining right angles and curves, helps to unify the four façades. At the same time these entrant angles stress the vertical pattern at the four corners exactly where the central and peripheral Mexican pyramids exaggerate the horizontal division into separate stages (plate 37). At the House of the Magician, Uxmal (plates 97, 98), a series of depressed masks links the simple unframed staircase of the pyramid to the main mass, reminiscent of E VII Sub. The base of the Uxmal pyramid is actually oval in plan, as the entrant angles have been submerged into the more flowing geometrical outline.

The towering pyramids at Tikal contrast with the lower, more massive design of another Maya type. Structure A-V at Uaxactún (plate 95), a good example, began with three temples on a single platform and grew into a complex series of temples, shrines, and palaces. At Piedras Negras (plate 81) the joining of different pyramids and platforms of the Acropolis into a complex unity is on an even larger scale and is reminiscent of the twentieth-century skyscraper city.

Maya temples are as rich and diverse as the pyramids. The cubical form appears at Uxmal (plate 97) and Chichén Itzá (plates 59, 62). Incredibly rich architectural sculpture sometimes has a baroque intensity; this is heightened by deep shadows which contrast with the sparkling high lights of mosaic reliefs above the plain undecorated lower walls. At Palenque in the Usumacinta River area (plates 75, 76) we find a group of elegant temples with delicate reliefs and highly pierced, towering roof combs. The outer edges of the vaults are cut back, in a form resembling the mansard roof of the last century, simultaneously giving an appearance of lightness and reducing the actual weight of the masonry vaults. At Tikal, on the other hand, the mass of masonry is increased to gargantuan proportions, while the interior is more a burrow than a space (plate 87). The central axis of the interior runs through a series of doorways that are both wider and deeper than the minute rooms they link. The rooms seem almost vestigial and remind one of closets. Whereas the temples at Palenque seem to minimize the volume of masonry, those at Tikal seem to minimize internal space.

The Toltec-influenced Castillo at Chichén Itzá (plates 59, 60), an example of Maya post-Classic temple-pyramid design, is

23

radially symmetrical with four staircases, one up each face, reminiscent of E VII Sub. It also calls to mind European comparisons, for instance the Villa Rotunda of Palladio (plate 61). Both works show the architect striving for a radially symmetrical plan and four similar elevations. At the Castillo one sees how almost transparent this aim is, for the temple on its four-faced pyramid consists of a single room, the standard Mesoamerican temple type, with an entrance of three openings on one side. The other three sides of the temple each have an entrance (of only one opening), and these three lead *not* into the main chamber, or cella, but into a corridor whose function is merely to provide the desired openings. The corridor does not even give direct access to the cella itself. The anonymous architect of the Castillo shaped the plan of the temple to conform to the symmetry of the pyramid plan and made the four façades of the temple similar through the repetition of the entrance motif. Close parallels between the two buildings, one Middle-American, one Italian Renaissance, both on platforms, both with four formal entrance staircases and four repeating façades, further demonstrate how the architects used similar means to achieve similar ends.

The combination of a small space-enclosing building with a solid and potentially inert architectural mass as support was remarkably flexible in the hands of the pre-Columbian architect. A change in the shape of the base could suggest solidity or towering elegance; a change in the proportions of the temple on top of the base could imply a large and spacious interior or heavy monumentality. The wall of the temple and the revetments covering the pyramid, however, never give the impression of being solid lifeless masses. By the various angles of slope and concentrated bands of ornament in sculpture and painting, the pyramid stages and temple walls were organized to avoid any such appearance of being inert. That this was important to the native builder is clear from early colonial paintings of temples in which the articulation of the walls is most specifically shown (plate 2).

24

The American pyramid is a monument of articulated mass fundamentally devoid of enclosed space. In contrast, the palace of central and peripheral Mexico is a group of rooms arranged around an enclosed space—a patio or courtyard. The contrast between the solid mass and the enclosed space is striking. Innumerable variations were wrought on the single theme of the pyramid; but although the palace as an architectural type is more restricted in the number of variations, the number of themes is larger.

No significant examples of palaces exist earlier than those of Teotihuacán (plates 39–41), where a fundamental type is defined. Following a design rare in European architectural history, the central patio is bounded by four independent building façades, linked at the recessed corners by subsidiary closing units. The space of the patio is thus closed, but the integrity of each façade of the four sides creating the enclosure is rigorously maintained at the expense of the unity of the whole. This type of architectural composition, best considered as a unitary design, is in contrast with those courtyards so common in the European tradition, where unified rows of columns and arches encircle the space of the patio with only a minor interruption, usually a change of direction at the corners. Unitary design of the Teotihuacán patio façades is similar to that of Teotihuacán pyramids, in which each stage maintains its integrity as a single unit. In both, it is only through the repetition of similar forms and the strong axial accent of the central staircase that the building design is brought into a compositional whole (plate 38).

Typically, the façades of the buildings surrounding the central patios of these Teotihuacán palaces have two columns *in antis* between extensions of the side walls of the building (plate 39), making a porch of three openings strongly reminiscent of the Greek megaron. The porch is approached by a staircase in line with the central opening; the whole is raised on a *talud* and *tablero* base. The linking corner units are set so far back that the patio seems to have open or at least deeply recessed corners. These corner units may in turn be bounded by colonnades similar in design but smaller in scale. Behind the porches are the rather small and simple square or rectangular rooms with flat ceilings supported by wooden beams. Many of the walls at Teotihuacán are articulated; the walls bounding the porches, for instance, divide into a low *talud* zone, and above it the major height of the wall functions as a *tablero*. These divisions are reinforced by the frescoes that decorate them—horizontal groups of figures on the *talud* (gods, striding priests, or animals) and an overall diaper pattern covering the rest of the surface functioning as a *tablero* (plates 41, 42). This twofold division of the wall stresses its unitary nature, which in turn echoes the unitary composition of the building platform and even the patio as a whole. [29]

The architects of the post-Classic site of Tula preferred another type of palace and patio design. In the so-called "Burned Palace" (plate 51) a series of rooms surrounds a rectangular patio which is defined by four continuous ranges of identical columns. Here there is no suggestion of a series of independent buildings brought together to define a patio; instead the patio has the effect of a single unified whole—a design later repeated in the Mercado of Toltec Chichén Itzá.[30]

Palaces of the Aztec period are less well known through excavations, but pictures of them drawn by natives soon after the Conquest are preserved in manuscripts of the early colonial period. The Mapa de Quinatzin (plate 3), in a drawing combining plan and elevation in one graphic system, shows the palace of Texcoco just before the Spanish Conquest. With due allowance for the native graphic conventions, this palace can be read as a unitary composition. The top of the sheet clearly shows a large building flanked on one side by a single building and on the other by a pair of smaller structures. The right and left sides of the patio are defined by two long buildings, and at the bottom of the page are small linking corner chambers similar to those from Teotihuacán (plate 39). The palace of Montezuma in México-Tenochtitlán, one of the most important of the Aztec palaces, is known only through inadequate descriptions and drawings, for, unfortunately, no significant archaeological work has been done on its site. The site, bordering the main plaza, or *zócalo*, of Mexico City, is presently occupied by the National Palace of Mexico, so that generalized literary accounts cannot be checked archaeologically against the remains (plate 15).[31]

The palaces at Mitla (plates 16–19), near Monte Albán in Oaxaca, have elements similar to both the systems of patio construction of Teotihuacán-Texcoco and of Tula. Inner patios are square and closed; although each face is an independent design, it is also linked with the façades adjacent to it. There are no recessed corners, and as there are no columns or piers, the effect is merely of an enclosed square unroofed room or space. These patios are not completely unified, nor are they composed of such discrete entities as to be absolutely unitary. If the Mitla plans were completely unified compositions, they would present an even more unbroken or more closely knit interior patio façade. Nevertheless, the palace plans (plate 16) indicate that whereas the interior patios are regular and almost unified in design, the exterior walls of the buildings may either enclose a solid rectangle in unified fashion or have the recessed corners associated with buildings of a unitary composition. The Mitla palaces are thus intermediaries between clearly unitary and purely unified designs. Mitla also has examples of groups of buildings constructed around a central enclosed area so that the individual buildings do not touch at the corners, and there are no subsidiary corner buildings to close the central space completely. These are best considered, however, as organizations of separate buildings around a plaza rather than as parts of a single building surrounding its patio.

In contrast, Maya palaces follow another principle. They stand one or more vaulted chambers deep, isolated upon platforms of considerable length. The Palace of the Governors at Uxmal (plate 102) with a double range of rooms is such a palace; Structure 51, South Acropolis, Tikal (plate 88), has four parallel rows of rooms. These palaces seem to have grown from simple structures into larger, more complex buildings by the addition of units in juxtaposition. There are palaces of only a single long row of rooms or of several units arranged around a large court; when they enclose a patio, other ranges of buildings sometimes seem to have been associated later with the first unit. In the Nunnery at Uxmal (plates 99–101), each of the four façades has a different design; one even has rooms on two levels. The patio of the Nunnery is thus considerably less unified that the Mitla patios (plate 18), where the scale of the buildings as well as the similar repeating patterns of the façades all help create the unified effect.

A fine example of Maya construction by accretion survives in Structure A–V at Uaxactún (plate 95). Careful excavation, drawings, and reconstructions[32] show clearly how this edifice, at first three temples, isolated units on a single platform, grew like a living organism into a complex of temples and palaces by constant rebuilding over several hundred years. In looking at Structure A-V in terms of its building history, one immediately senses its dynamic quality; it never ceased to grow until it finally died.

The great palace at Palenque, "El Palacio" (plates 79, 80), is another example of this organic aspect of Maya palaces, quite comparable to the onionskin growth of the pyramid. The palace consists of a series of long buildings with parallel lines of rooms and patios among them. It is filled with elegant architectural sculpture in stone and stucco. Dominating all is a single four-story tower, unique in Middle America. The palace at Río Bec (plate 83) and those at related sites such as Xpuhil also have towers, but they are merely solid, impenetrable masses of masonry. Designed as false temples on false pyramids, they are mere decorative addenda to the building, unlike the Palenque Tower, which has a complete interior staircase.[33]

The purpose of the palaces of Teotihuacán (plates 39–42), Tula (plate 51), and of the Aztec period (plates 3, 15) seems clearly to have been for residence. At Mitla (plates 16–19) the palaces may have had a more strictly religious function; at Calixtlahuaca the palace type building may have been a priestly school, or *calmecac* (plate 7). The function of the Maya palace is, however, undecided among scholars, who seem loath to admit they could have been residences for members of the priestly hierarchy. Another possibility—that they were used for aspects of the cult such as fasting, penance of the priests, and storage of paraphernalia—would give them the same relation to the main temples that the sacristies, chapels, and baptistries of the Christian tradition bear to the church to which they are attached. The sequence from three temples to a palace complex in Structure A–V at Uaxactún (plate 95) supports this interpretation with added chronological implications. Probably both theories contain elements of the truth.

ARCHITECTURAL SCULPTURE AND PAINTING

The total visual effect of the temple on its pyramid or of the palace on its platform was not only the result of architectural design as read in plan, elevation, and cross sections. Nor was it due solely to the characteristics of external massing and internal space, or even to the relationships among buildings produced by careful city planning. An additional and important factor was the plastic treatment of surfaces with sculpture and the chromatic embellishment with painting. The larger aspects of architecture were typically a crude rubble core done "in the rough" and covered with a carefully worked facing. This facing, or outer skin, could be a series of carved stone slabs or, as at Mitla (plate 19), a stone mosaic. Stucco could also be modeled in high and low relief, as at Palenque (plates 77, 78). In all cases the final surface was probably polychromed or at least painted white, and this would be even more definite in cases of the architectural sculpture. In addition to these uses, painting existed in its own right as mural painting, examples of which have been discovered at Teotihuacán (plates 41, 42), Tizatlán, near Tlaxcala, from the late pre-Conquest period, and Chichén Itzá, Tulum, and Bonampak (plates 55, 56) from the Maya area.

Sculpture also had a double role; it was both an attribute of, and a decoration for, architecture. Pre-Classic E VII Sub at Uaxactún (plate 92) can be considered architecture decorated with sculptured masks, or it can with equal validity be judged as a sculpture of monumental proportions. Planar and mass relationships unite the steps, stairs, and masks in this first major known work of Maya architecture, sharply contrasting with the more strictly architectural simplicity of Cuicuilco (plate 9)—the early pyramid from the central Valley of Mexico.

In the Classic period at Teotihuacán (plates 37, 38) the architect did not build with the idea that "form follows function." Rather, he projected the *tableros* from the wall in an almost precarious manner. At El Tajín (plate 11) construction of the niches was so unfunctional that they easily fell into ruin. The architect solved structural problems as well as he could, secure in the knowledge that the devices resorted to would not show; all would be covered with a stucco veneer. Architectural truth lay in the end itself not in the means employed to achieve it.

Teotihuacán offers the interesting example of the Pyramid of Quetzalcoatl in the Citadel (plate 38), where a series of richly carved *tableros* with great projecting serpent heads and "obsidian butterflies" alternate above *taluds* alive with undulating serpents and sea shells. All were discarded or covered by a later construction of painted *tableros* and *taluds* in simple planes (plate 37). Fragmentary remains indicate that the later building was painted in striking and bold designs. At Teotihuacán painting had superseded sculpture.

The post-Classic relief panels on the Pyramid of Tlahuizcalpantecuhtli (plates 45, 46) at Tula show felines, birds, and mythical monsters. The banquette in some sections still has its original color and suggests the original polychromy of the pyramid—dark red, white, ocher, blue, yellow, and green. Color emphasized the simplicity of the clear low relief forms. One by one, the creatures stand isolated from the background along their frieze. Gone are the interweaving motifs of the Teotihuacán Quetzalcoatl pyramid *tableros*. The wall of snakes, or *coatepantli*, surrounding the Pyramid of Tenayuca (plates 27, 28) was both polychromed and sculptured. The snakes, though separate, are placed

29

so that they touch, thereby creating a pattern in which the elements are neither discrete and unitary, as at Tula, nor complex and interwoven, as at Teotihuacán. The Tenayuca snakes combine roughly carved stone heads with bodies modeled in mortar set with a rough mosaic of small stones. The whole was stuccoed and painted over so that the distinction which we now see between modeled and carved forms was absent when the pieces were finished.[34] The sculptor as well as the architect covered his tracks with paint and plaster.

Pre-Classic relief sculpture at Monte Albán in peripheral Mexico survives in the dancing figures from the Pyramid of the Danzantes (plate 23). The curvilinear fluid forms, carved on slabs of irregular shape, form an early retaining wall covered by the later pyramid. Others are built into the back walls of the Observatory (plate 24). Their style suggests a relationship between Monte Albán and the early enigmatic "Olmec culture,"[35] a culture which is in turn related to the masks of E VII Sub at Uaxactún (plate 92). Other than the Danzantes there is little stone sculpture at Monte Albán.[36]

The palaces at nearby Mitla (plates 16–19), like the pyramids of Monte Albán, are constructed with a series of hanging *tableros*; their overlapping forms suggest either a massive wall with successive layers peeled away to reveal underlying layers of rich design or a series of forms applied one over another to an existing wall. These hanging *tableros* are decorated with elaborate patterns worked in mosaics of small pieces of stone and based fundamentally on the patterns of textiles. It is as though the walls were covered with a series of *serapes* hanging like tapestries over the face of the *tablero*, in contrast to the *talud* below, left relatively simple.

The Temple of Xochicalco (plate 52) was covered with a revetment of carved slabs in low relief. Unlike the carved slabs at Tula, the area of the slab and the area of the design units here were not coterminous, yet the individual slabs are too large to be considered parts of a mosaic. The *talud*, more spacious than those of Teotihuacán, has a great feathered serpent which suggests the Quetzalcoatl motifs at Teotihuacán (plate 38). The pose and elaborate headdress of one seated figure seems almost to be a provincial version of Maya figures, while the hooks and scrolls radiating from the serpent have formal affiliations with sculptures from El Tajín (double outlines and lattice panels provide additional similarities). This sculpture has a cosmopolitan, if not an eclectic, look about it.

At Malinalco (plate 12) where buildings are carved out of the mountain itself, we are dealing not with architectural sculpture but rather with sculptured architecture. It is interesting to notice here that the subsidiary sculpture, moveable and lost from other sites, remains intact, still attached to the mother rock. The doorway, carved into the mouth of the earth monster, gives valuable evidence, even though it may be aberrant, of how this crucial architectural focal point was treated in at least one temple. Even more than Teopanzalco (plate 31), Malinalco preserves the form of the native temple.

Maya architectural sculpture at Uxmal (plates 97–102) in the Puuc region of Yucatán, is elaborated on the vault zone above the smooth flat surface of the wall level. High relief composed in mosaic fashion breaks up the great mass of the masonry vaults by creating patterns of light and shade to contrast with the unvaried light on the flat wall below. The zone of decoration includes mosaic background diaper patterns of diagonal lattices and closely spaced short semicylindrical forms suggesting balusters or the saplings of the wall of the Maya house. Against these background patterns house forms are silhouetted (plate 101), stylized double-headed serpents pile up, and great masks mark doorways. But richness is always governed by a control; simple surfaces or repeat patterns are invariably used to set off concentrations of sculpture. The richness of Maya decoration is further seen at Hochob (plate 73) with its entire façade covered by a single great mosaic mask. At Río Bec (plate 83) sculptured false temples and pyramids are used as the decorative motifs of great towers rising from palace-type constructions in *double entendre* plays upon design elements. Doors pierced through mouths and whole buildings reduced to architectural sculpture suggest a world of fantasy and the grotesque.

At Tikal (plates 85–87) isolated masks in the vault zone of the temples are concentrations of ornament supplemented by elaborately carved wooden lintels on a smaller scale and towering carved roof combs. Here architecture again suggests sculpture. Further south, at Copán (plates 68, 69), the carved relief risers of the Hieroglyphic Staircase are decorated with the longest inscription in Maya "writing" known to us. Sculpture in this case has become epigraphy. Copán has other examples of epigraphy as sculptural motif in its stele. These great stone monuments, usually with a richly garbed human figure on one side and calendrical inscriptions on the back, serve to relate the temples they front to the plazas they punctuate and to locate temples, plazas, and even the site as a whole to the cosmos. Made to be viewed from all sides, the stele suggest European monumental free-standing sculpture, but their function in the plan of the site as a whole is quite clearly architectural.[37]

Stele N (761 A.D.) from Copán is illustrated by an engraving from Stephens' pioneering travel book in the Maya area (plate 72). Catherwood's delightful and somewhat romantic illustrations for this book are so accurate that they can be used to reconstruct details lost since the lithographs were published in the first half of the nineteenth century.[38] A comparison between Stele N and Stele 12 (795 A.D.) from Piedras Negras (plate 82) indicates the wide range of artistic expression used in Maya stele. The Copán work is so plastic, so carefully designed to create patterns of light and shade as it stood in an open plaza in the full light of the southern sun, so exuberant in the proliferation of detail over its surface, and so integrated into an artistic unity imbued with an incipient drama, that we are justified in referring to it as an example of the late development of an old style. The Piedras Negras Stele 12, in lower relief, is more dramatic in terms of the situation portrayed but less filled with the drama that comes from more purely artistic means of expression. It has a fineness and restraint lacking in the Copán stele and indicates a more refined taste and sensitive handling of sculptural surfaces. The back and sides of the Maya stele have long calendrical inscriptions where the date signs pile up almost like the building stones of a wall, paralleling on a smaller scale the great Hieroglyphic Staircase of inscriptions at Copán (plate 69).

If the Copán stele suggests seventeenth-century European baroque sculpture, the delicate stuccoed interior of a room in House E of the palace at Palenque (plate 77) is surely reminiscent of the eighteenth-century rococo style. Delicately modeled curvilinear plants hang pendant from a molding separating the wall from the vault surface. Asymmetry, subtle but present, gives this stucco relief the vitality we see in the drawings made for Maudslay's publication[39] and reflects the rococo nature of stucco cartouches in House A from the palace group. Pier F from House D of the palace, slightly but accurately restored in the drawing (plate 78), shows a warrior seizing a prisoner by the hair and about to strike him with an ax—an ax more floral than lethal, a blow more from the ballet than from combat. The standing figure is placed on a ground line of vegetal exuberance, and the captive wears great pendant earrings which echo the necklace of the standing figure and the regular pattern of the frame around the whole composition.

Chichén Itzá, whose close connections with Tula are documented in historical writings, also shows remarkable similarity of architectural sculpture. For instance, round columns of human form (plates 47, 48) and square columns covered with low relief (plates 49, 63) are found at both sites. Similar hanging *tableros* with relief sculpture adorn the Pyramid of Tlahuizcalpantecuhtli at Tula (plates 45, 46) and the Venus Platform at Chichén Itzá (plate 65). Chacmols (plate 66), statues of recumbent men with their heads turned toward the spectator, are part of the religious furniture of both sites. At Chichén Itzá certain elements—great stone mosaic masks—appear on the walls of the Toltec-period Temple of the Warriors (plates 62, 63), and relate both to Uxmal (plates 97, 100, 101) and to pre-Toltec buildings at Chichén Itzá itself. The Castillo (plates 59, 60), often used to characterize Chichén Itzá, is actually different from most buildings at the site because of its radial symmetry and almost puritanical lack of architectural sculpture; it relies for architectural effect upon simple cubical mass and uncarved hanging *tableros*.

Relatively few examples of architectural painting—mural painting rather than painting as a finish for architectural sculpture—have survived, but they indicate the vast amount of impressive work missing from our view of pre-Hispanic American art. The main examples of Classic times are from Teotihuacán in the central Valley of Mexico (plates 41, 42) and Bonampak from the Maya area (plates 55, 56). In central Mexico the remaining post-Classic murals are few, fragmentary, or minor; the principal work among them is an altar at Tizatlán near Tlaxcala[40]. From the Maya area impressive remains of post-Classic murals were found at Tulum and Chichén Itzá, but essentially they show a decline from the high quality of the Bonampak examples.

Murals from Atetelco at Teotihuacán (plates 41, 42) come from the porch of a palace group and follow the pattern of many Teotihuacán murals. The architect articulated the wall in a way similar to that used to articulate the steps of the pyramid; a lower inclined zone recalls the *talud*, and an upper vertical plane suggests the *tablero*. The painter seems to have followed this division. On the lower zone the figures may be in a procession or in a symmetrical balanced composition, but their design is controlled by the low sloping section of wall they are painted on.

In the upper zone the pattern seems close to wallpaper in its aesthetic function, for it is essentially a repeating design, lacking the symmetry of the processional groups in the lower zone.[41]

The paintings of both zones follow the dictates governing much of what is called "primitive" art. Generally speaking, figures are distinguished by a strong outline, and within this outline colors are applied in solid flat areas with no indication of shading.[42] Overlapping of one form by another is avoided as much as possible, and the parts of the human body are shown in their broadest or most typical aspect; for example, heads, legs, and feet are in profile, body in full front view. As a concomitant of these limitations upon the human figure, poses and positions tend to be limited and stereotyped. No attempt is made to give the illusion of three-dimensional space; what is assumed to be farther back in space is shown above what is assumed to be closer. Taken together, these are the characteristics of a conceptual art, a mode of painting and sculpture wherein the artist paints or models in terms of a series of concepts he holds about objects in nature. It is in contrast with the perceptual mode, where the artist aims at re-creating the things he perceives.

These features of conceptual art result in an essentially unitary composition, whereas perceptual art tends to be more unified. It is interesting to note that the painting, like the architecture, of Teotihuacán is unitary in composition, and that central and peripheral Mexican art has a logical consistency in both architecture and mural painting, indicating that these New World peoples had in a very real sense a comprehensive artistic style with significant regional and temporal subdivisions.

Even in the mural of the "Earthly Paradise" or "Tlalocan," at Tepantitla in Teotihuacán, a mural more perceptual and unified than the paintings at Atetelco from the same site, the artist was still working within the framework of primitive conventions to a remarkable degree. Space is two dimensional; what is behind is shown above; line bounds forms tightly; the distribution of forms on the surface is governed by the horror vacui and leads to the even sifting of forms upon the wall surface. In its air of general animation and its more complex range and interrelationships of figures, the control of unitary design is weakened but still present. At Tepantitla painting and architecture still are part of a single artistic style, and this unitary style of painting reflects the unitary nature of the architecture it embellishes.

Murals at Bonampak (plate 55) show how much further

34

toward the perceptual native painters had gone in the Maya area. Remarkably unified in design, these murals were planned, like the Teotihuacán frescoes, as integral parts of the architecture. The design was adjusted for differences in height so that figures at eye-level seem almost to be parts of a *talud*, while the upper figures on the soffit of the vault suggest the *tablero*. The composition flows smoothly from one wall of the building to the next so that this linking of all four walls is reminiscent of the way the stairs are bound to the pyramid by masks at Uxmal (plates 97, 98) or the way the four faces of a Maya pyramid are often linked by the series of entrant angles and curves at the four corners of the plan (plate 87). In comparison with central and peripheral Mexico, the greater unity in Maya painting reflects the greater unity in Maya architecture.

The frescoes of Teotihuacán and Bonampak demonstrate that the mural painting of Middle America can truly be considered "architectural painting." Basically this style was two-dimensional and well adapted to decorate a wall without destroying or even threatening its integrity as a flat enclosing plane. Architecture and painting retain the same relative degree of unitary and unified composition.

CITY PLANS

The remarkably cohesive and consistent plans of individual Middle American cities, as they exist now, demonstrate that the sum total of the aesthetic effect of a Pre-Columbian city was greater than its individual parts—the buildings, plazas, and avenues. At the same time they indicate that cities were not built according to single preconceived plans drawn up early in their histories to which all subsequent building conformed. Instead, the congruency of parts in Middle American cities seems to come from a consistent series of architectural decisions made in response to architectural problems continually arising when each subsequent building was to be built. These additions seem to indicate a plan becoming increasingly more unified and less unitary in the course of time, since later buildings were absorbed harmoniously into the existing pattern. The result is apt to appear as though there were a more unifying plan throughout the history of the site than was actually the case.

Two main principles of organization dominate city plans in ancient America. One is axial, where the buildings are organized along a central axis, creating longitudinal relationships in varying degrees of dynamic tension and impelling the beholder to movement through the composition. The other principle is that of enclosure, where there is either a central motif or motifs around which buildings are grouped, or a group of architectural units which enclose a central space. The earliest known example of each principle in central Mexico appears at Teotihuacán.

The Teotihuacán site as a whole is organized along a great axis now called the "Avenue of the Dead," the Miccaotli (plate 33), ending to the north in a plaza subordinate to the Pyramid of the Moon.[43] The larger Pyramid of the Sun (plates 34 and 35) is on the east side of the main axis to the south. The Citadel (plate 36) is also on the east side of the axis, but even further south. Both the great pyramids are given architectural settings in the plan by subsidiary buildings which form plazas linking the mass of the pyramid to the central axis. The Pyramid of the Moon is linked directly to the north end of the avenue by its plaza, while the axis of the plaza in front of the Pyramid of the Sun crosses the Avenue of the Dead to establish a movement at right angles to the axis of the site as a whole.[44]

The enclosing principle underlies the Citadel, a great rectangular platform surrounding a completely enclosed sunken plaza. The four sides of this platform have smaller pyramids. Dominating the far side and facing the Avenue of the Dead across the sunken plaza is the Pyramid of Quetzalcoatl (plates 37, 38). In the center of the Citadel plaza a small square platform with a staircase up each of its four sides acts as a focal point for the enclosed space. Thus the design is partially centralized, with the central platform functioning as the obelisk of a baroque plaza, or as George Kubler has recently called it, a cairn.[45] The central focus is emphasized by the Pyramid of Quetzalcoatl, for this building turns its main façade to one side of the plaza and acts as the eastern boundary of the enclosed space. At the same time it sets one side of the surrounding platform apart from the others, implying a cross-axis linking it through the small central platform to the Avenue of the Dead, a cross-axis parallel to the one linking the Pyramid of the Sun to the main axis. The platforms creating the sunken plaza may very well be later additions to the complex, indicating that the original Quetzalcoatl pyramid was related to the site axis much as the Pyramid of the Sun is now. Furthermore, the platforms creating the sunken plaza have the same elevation as the later addition to the Quetzalcoatl pyramid (plate 37) and are thus distinct from the rich, elaborately carved façades of the earlier pyramid.

The great site from peripheral Mexico in the Classic period is Monte Albán (plates 20, 21). Like Teotihuacán, this site now has a dominant plan. It is organized around a great rectangular central plaza closed on the north and south ends by raised platforms, and on the east and west sides, by ranges of buildings. Instead of a small square platform as the focal point, this giant main plaza has a rectangular group of three buildings in the center. A fourth building, the Observatory (plate 24), is earlier and seems to be a legacy from a previous building phase, for it does not fit into the plan as coherently as the other three buildings. The North Platform (plate 25), separated from the main space by a columnar screen, has an approximately square sunken plaza; in the center of the plaza is a small square platform which is similar to that of the Citadel at Teotihuacán.

A detail from a post-Classic Mixtec manuscript (plate 1) also shows such a centralized composition. Five temples on platforms of varying height surround a motif in the center of a plaza—a wooden drill with a fireboard and the symbol for fire coming from it. This fire might have been kindled on a low four-sided platform of the type found in the central plaza of the Citadel at Teotihuacán (plate 36) or the North Platform at Monte Albán (plate 25). It is interesting to notice the plan of a ball court behind the plaza to the left. At Monte Albán the ball court (plate 26) is one of the structures bounding the main plaza to the east.

The central spine of buildings at Monte Albán, excluding the observatory (j on plate 21), is on a north-south axis, linking these buildings to the staircase of the South Platform, a staircase related to neither of the mounds on this platform. This axis bends when it connects the most northern of the central buildings with the North Platform. The central plaza of the North Platform, like the two pyramids of the South Platform, does not line up with this axis. This discrepancy is masked at one end by the off-center staircase of the South Platform and, at the other, by the colonnaded entrance porch, or propylaeum, of the North Platform. The two staircases leading to the propylaeum are not on the major axis either, nor even on a single axis. A plausible explanation is that the propylaeum was built to mask the deviation of the major axis between the major plaza and the sunken plaza of the North Platform.

If this explanation is valid, one can see at Monte Albán the hand of an architect of genius who attempted to bring the whole site into a pattern of axial unity, overcoming the irregularity that reigned before he built the propylaeum. It is also possible that other changes were made in an attempt to regularize the plan. Buildings IV and m on the west side of the main plaza flanking the Danzantes pyramid reflect these changes. Both buildings are pyramids with forecourts formed by extended side walls and closed by subsidiary platforms in front; the subsidiary platforms are reminiscent of the platform supporting the propylaeum which closes off the north sunken plaza. The effect of these platforms is to narrow the space between the west buildings and the buildings of the central spine, making this space closer in width to the space on the east side. An interesting aspect of these buildings is their position; they are not oriented east and west to conform to the north-south axis of the central spine, but, like the Observatory, they seem to have been placed in a more or less arbitrary fashion. Since buildings IV and m probably were built before the aim for greater axial unity, these forecourts were perhaps attempts to bring them into closer relationship with the rest of the site while the plan was still evolving.

Tula (plates 43, 44, 50), of the post-Classic period, was designed with a colonnade on parts of two sides of its plaza, a colonnade emphasized to such an extent that it screens the façade of the Pyramid of Tlahuizcalpantecuhtli. Like the circumscribing mound of the Citadel at Teotihuacán or the buildings around the central plaza at Monte Albán, the colonnade encloses the space, producing a self-contained effect. This architectural group functions as a centralized composition rather than as the linear, axial composition of the Avenue of the Dead at Teotihuacán. In its center is a low four-sided platform similar to the focal structures at both Monte Albán and the Citadel of Teotihuacán.[46]

In contrast with the four-sided platform acting as the focus or obelisk in a plaza is the Aztec pyramid (plates 29, 31). Its rectangular plan, twin staircases, and the two temples side by side at the top all create the impression of blocking off space in front from space behind, so that it acts as a parenthesis rather than as an obelisk. Although it can mark the end of an axis or one side of a plaza, it cannot function as the focal center for enclosed space.

The four-sided platform in the center of a plaza can be compared to the Parthenon in architectural effect. The Parthenon, with its open colonnade surrounding the cella, admits the view equally from all angles; open on all sides, neither end façade is compellingly the main one. In contrast, the Aztec temple is frontal, raised upon a base in much the same way as the Maison

Carrée at Nîmes (plate 32). Like the Roman temple, entrance is limited to one face, and this is clearly defined as the front. The back and the two sides of both buildings are closed off visually as well as physically; there is no possible peripheral approach. The preferred approach to both is through a rectangular plaza.

The center of México-Tenochtitlán (plates 13, 15) consisted of a great rectangular religious plaza surrounded by a *coatepantli*, or snake wall, broken by four entrances; these were the ends of causeways leading from Ixtapalapa, Tepeaca, and Tlacopan (Tacuba). The fourth entrance was the road which began at a landing stage for canoes, a point of embarkation to the opposite shore of the lake. Within this armature of four roads the remainder of the city was divided into four main quarters. Tlatelolco, formerly an independent city-state until conquered by the people of México-Tenochtitlán, was itself divided into additional subdivisions.[47] These divisions of the city were organized into a gridiron plan; streets and canals ran at right angles to each other, with occasional diagonals interrupting the regularity.[48] Each of the subdivisions had, in turn, its own religious center and its own pyramid and temples with accompanying plazas. Minor temples seem to have been built in addition to these more important ones.

The written sources of the plan of the capital are meager, but a careful reading of the documents in conjunction with the early sixteenth-century Plano en Papel de Maguey makes it clear that México-Tenochtitlán was not a formless urban conglomeration of buildings. Even the fringes of the Pre-Columbian city consisted of cultivated land intersected by a gridiron pattern of roads and canals most likely similar to the *chinampas*, or "floating gardens," still to be seen along the shores of the lake at Xochimilco.[49]

The representative Maya city plan uses the same two basic themes as Mexican city planning, and gives them a rich series of variations. At Tikal (plate 84) we see both themes combined, for here centralizing plazas are constructed at each end of a monumental causeway (*sacbe*). One side of each plaza—the side facing the causeway—is open. Here the axial nature of the causeway acts as a link between the two otherwise closed plazas. The plazas, with their centralizing characteristics, are treated as a single space split, as it were, and at the same time are linked by the longitudinal axis established by the *sacbe*.

The Acropolis at Piedras Negras (plate 81) shows the enclosure of a great plaza by frontally designed buildings and the use of a colonnade as a propylaeum leading from one plaza into another, suggesting the propylaeum of Monte Albán. It also shows another important Maya device for achieving harmonious relationships among buildings: differences of level among the constituent parts. The main plaza at one level is followed by a higher plaza, followed in turn by another closed plaza surrounded by palace structures at a still higher level. These Maya building complexes are composed of temples on pyramids and palaces on platforms. Spaces before important buildings may be punctuated by stele echoing the broken skyline, which is a series of contrasts between the flat long lines of palace roofs and high vertical accents of pyramids and temples. Just as plaza leads into plaza and stele leads to temple, so temple links to palace, and palace to temple.

Palenque (plate 74) provides another example of the extensive Maya city and shows the interrelationship of palace and temple buildings. Structure A-V at Uaxactún (plate 95) starts with three early temples on a single platform and gradually evolves into a later complex dominated by palace-type structures, indicating that the changing emphasis on temples, palaces, and closed plazas may have chronological implications in the design of Maya cities. The palaces, with their long ranges of vaulted rooms surrounding sunken plazas, often have only limited passage from one side through to the other. Thus they might very well have been used for military defense. They surround and dominate the sunken plazas, which may have functioned as places of last resort in warfare.[50] This view is compatible with the situation in central Mexico, where the temple on its platform was just such a place of last resort (plate 2). It was not until the post-Classic period that proper defensive walls were built around cities like Mayapán and Tulum (plate 91). This overt military element added to city planning probably represents an architectural reaction to changing patterns of warfare.

Post-Classic Maya architecture, best represented at Chichén Itzá, shows the influence of the Toltec invaders from Tula in the similarity of the colonnade in front of the Temple of the Warriors (plate 62) to the colonnade from Tula (plates 44, 50). The use of a plaza partially enclosed by a colonnade would suggest a radially symmetrical building in its center. At Tula there is such a building in the low four-sided radially symmetrical central platform (plate 43). At Chichén Itzá the Castillo provides the focus for a colonnaded plaza (plate 58). The position of the Castillo clearly indicates why the architect forced the Middle American temple, essentially frontal, into a radially symmetrical pattern in this building. The Castillo is, as it were, comparable to the central platform of the sunken plazas at Monte Albán and the Citadel at Teotihuacán, raised to monumental proportions.

It is interesting to consider effects upon the visitor of the two types of plan. The central plan impels him to look about, to walk around the central motif, but it does not encourage him to leave the shelter of the enclosing space. The axial plan, however, is quite different, for it suggests things in the distance; it leads him from one unit to the next along its length. In this respect it is more dynamic than the central plan. Maya variants on both themes are more common than either theme in its pure state, and the combination of both can be seen where roads lead into otherwise enclosed plazas or where a sequence of enclosed plazas can even suggest an axial arrangement as the visitor passes from one plaza into another (Piedras Negras, plate 81).

Maya cities are more sophisticated and varied in the ordering of their buildings, plazas, and roads than the cities of central Mexico, just as other aspects of Maya architecture express the longer period of evolution and more highly cultivated civilization of the Maya. But the underlying principles of architecture, sculpture, painting, and city planning of Middle America can be deduced more surely from the simpler, more direct artistic statement of central Mexico than from the richer, more complex, and longer traditions of the Maya.

The Conquest of the areas of high civilization in the Andean region and the adjacent coast began in 1532, a little more than a decade after the Conquest of Mexico. Pizarro, the conqueror of Peru, and his men were better prepared for the wonders they were to see than Cortés and his followers had been, for this was the second time the Spaniards were to overthrow such a civilization.

Cuzco, capital of the Incas,[51] was cradled in a pleasant and prosperous valley high in the forbidding Andes. No painted and stuccoed plaster here, for Cuzco was built of solid massive walls of carefully cut masonry—stonework that seemed to grow out of the very earth, built to last for all time. Even today one can see narrow streets in Cuzco lined with precision-cut granite blocks (plate 110). The palaces of the Incas, rulers of the land, and the palaces of the nobility have all left their traces in modern Cuzco, where the same narrow streets are lined with the same formidable walls that once protected the gold and silver of the Inca and the treasures of the Temple of the Sun (plate 109).

Pizarro found the strife-torn empire of the Inca trying to bind up the wounds of recent civil war and was able to use the forces of dissension to help him destroy the Inca. The organization of the Empire of the Inca was extremely rigid. At the head was the Inca himself, below him a series of nobles, members of the royal family or rulers of conquered states. Below them were ranks of lesser officials, all subject to the ruler through a chain of command that kept strict control over even the most minor aspect of life in the realm. Religion was a part of the state, as one would expect with such a centralized society, and paralleled the interrelation of religion and government in the Mexico of Montezuma. The cult of the Sun God, Inti, was the state religion, and the Inca himself was held to be related to the Sun. Conquered states were allowed to keep their own religion and gods, but made to accept the Sun God. Temples to the Sun God were at the same time honors to the Inca, and they were built in all cities subject to his rule. Virgins consecrated to the cult, called the Chosen Ones and drawn from among the beautiful women of the realm, attended these temples.[52]

Cuzco is located in what is now Peru. It was the center and focus of a state extending from northern Chile through part of Bolivia and as far north as Ecuador. Peru is a land of contrasts: of towering mountains—the Andes; arid deserts—the Paracas Peninsula; a great highland lake—Lake Titicaca; of dead cities—Chanchan; and of old cities still living—Cuzco; of exotic animals—the alpaca, llama, and vicuña; and of uncountable treasures of silver and gold mined from the earth. The peoples who created a whole series of highly civilized states still live on in their descendants, for almost half the inhabitants of Peru today are Indians, speakers of Aymara or Quechua, the language of the Incas.

The land is divided between highlands and coastal regions. Archaeologists subdivide them further into northern, central, and southern areas. The highlands, even higher than the central Valley of Mexico, made their mark upon agriculture, the people, and the architecture. The climate is so cold in the highest places of human settlement that only a few plants such as the potato will grow (but not corn); the valleys of the mountain streams are so narrow and steep that hillsides have to be terraced to make fields. The Pre-Columbian dwellers along the coast lived in the lower valleys formed by streams draining the mountain highlands, places where little or no rain fell, but where the land could be made fertile with elaborate irrigation systems, utilizing the water from the mountains before it was swallowed up by thirsty desert sands or lost in the Pacific Ocean (see page 114).

Like the agriculture and the people, Andean architecture was influenced by geography. In the highlands, where stone was plentiful and construction was needed to protect against the cold and heavy rains, ashlar or rubble stone masonry was preferred; adobe (sun-dried brick) was used more sparingly. In the lowlands, where rainfall was less and adobe was reasonably permanent, it was preferred. The arid desert preserved the mud-brick architecture and the bodies of the people who built it. Bodies of the dead, wrapped in elaborate winding sheets, are still intact because of natural mummification. These textile wrappings of the dead are among the most handsome and technically proficient examples of weaving in its many techniques that man has ever made (plates 105, 107, 121).[53]

The history of the high cultures of Peru, like the history of Mexico, exists on two levels. It is known in its early phases only through archaeological evidence and reconstruction based on

43

artifacts. Later periods are known in greater detail through colonial accounts written in European script and based upon native traditions. The earlier periods of archaeological history are recorded in terms of five chronological divisions. The first, called the *Early Farmer*, describes a level of technology, and the second, *Cultist*, refers to widespread religious cults uniting many separate sites. A technological amplification of manufacturing techniques and a diversity of artistic forms characterizes the *Experimenter*, while the next period, the *Master Craftsman*, is the culmination of the earlier technological experiments. The *Expansionist* period refers to a time when influences from Tiahuanaco (plates 119, 120) radiated from that important center in the south highlands, and disorders attendant upon widespread warfare upset the patterns of living throughout the Andean region.[54]

Traditional history, as we know it from written sources, begins with accounts of the *City Builder* stage.[55] The native histories tell of the Chimu dominion on the north coast from their capital city of Chanchan (plates 103, 104, 106) in the Moche Valley. Central coast valleys made up the Cuismancu Empire, and further south the Chincha Empire was the powerful state on the coast.[56] All these independent states fell one by one to the imperialist energy of the Incas, whom the Spaniards found ruling the whole area.

The early architectural history, recorded only in archaeology, begins with the Castillo at Chavín de Huántar from the *Cultist* period. This building enunciated principles dominating the architecture of the highlands in Peru until the time of the Spanish Conquest. It is large both in plan (245 by 235 feet) and in elevation (45 feet high). Constructed of cut stone, the Castillo consists of a series of internal galleries and rooms with ventilating shafts lined with masonry, the whole set in a mass of rubble and faced externally with carefully cut stone.[57] The exterior has a decorative cornice and sculptured heads set into the wall with tenons. The *lanzón* (plate 108) gives an idea of the formal hieratic style dominating most Peruvian architectural sculpture. Linear patterns define a fantastic face, in this instance carved on a great prism of stone set inside one of the galleries. The style is gravely conceptual, reducing the forms of nature to severely stylized patterns of great expressive power.

The pyramids of the Sun and Moon at Moche, near the city of Trujillo on the north coast, are from the *Master Craftsman*

44

period and establish a principle of long duration in coastal architecture. The Temple of the Sun (plate 114), called locally the Huaca del Sol, is built of adobe brick. The structure is impressive because of its size; a platform of five terraces 750 feet long, 450 feet wide, and 60 feet high, with an access ramp on the northern face, it is crowned with a pyramid 340 feet square, rising an additional 75 feet in height.

This great mass of sun-dried brick is composed of a series of square piers or columns almost like a series of independent towers, not bonded together and indicating in their separateness the possibility that they were built by different groups of workers. Kubler has suggested a system whereby unskilled laborers delivered quotas of material for the construction, which would imply a highly organized social system.[58]

The Mochica society which built these monuments, according to the evidence of figures painted on Mochica pottery, was organized with a strong sacerdotal class governing a subordinate agricultural population. Among the interesting evidences of Mochica life are pottery house models (plate 115) which show that the Mochica house included a system of peaked and lean-to roofs with openings under the rafters for the circulation of air, so important in the hot climate. Agriculture in this arid region was carried on by means of large-scale irrigation systems which used water from the Moche River.

Tiahuanaco in the south highlands is the representative site of the *Expansionist* period. On the shores of Lake Titicaca, at an elevation of almost 13,000 feet, the site is vast. Here, as at Chavín, one finds carefully worked stone and impressive architectural sculpture. Calasasaya at this site had a masonry wall containing sufficient earth fill to make a great platform 445 feet by 425 feet, with a sunken court 196 feet by 131 feet. The raised earthwork has been reduced by erosion, but some stone revetments are still in place. A megalithic staircase and the Gate of the Sun (plates 119, 120) are the most striking remains at the site.

The Gate of the Sun, a monolith of andesite, is 10 feet high and 12½ feet wide, weighing about 10 tons. The upper part of this impressive piece of architectural sculpture has a band of forty-eight small figures carved in low relief, flanking a larger relief figure of a god, probably Viracocha, the Creator (plate 120). The smaller repeating figures strongly suggest the influence of textile designs in their regularity and harsh angularity (plate 121). The central figure, its chill stiffness looming over the smaller ones, might also have come from a woven source. In contrast to these figures is the opening, or doorway, beneath. This has a suggestion of elegance in its narrow recessed frame, composed of a lintel unit and two vertical jambs linked by a stepped juncture. Another smaller doorway at Tiahuanaco has a simpler frieze of sculpture but the same sensitive relation of architectural elements in the relief frame around the opening. A third doorway exhibits the architectural forms with no sculptured frieze at all. Skill in stone carving as well as fineness of design characterizes the work at this site.

Chanchan on the north coast dates from the *City Builder* phase of Peruvian architectural history and points out how appropriately this period is named. This great city, over six square miles in area, is a series of ten rectangular compounds, some as large as forty acres (plates 103, 104). Each contains houses with gabled roofs, pyramids, gardens, and reservoirs enclosed with one or as many as three walls. Remains of these walls as high as 30 feet still stand in the ruins (plate 106). Construction at Chanchan follows the coast tradition of adobe brick. Mosaics of adobe bricks make patterns on the walls, and a thick layer of mud laid on the walls was cut away to make arabesques suggestive of textile patterns so important for Peruvian designers in all the arts, ranging from nonrepresentational motifs to fish, birds, or animals (plate 107).[59]

Chanchan was the capital of a Chimu Empire stretching as far north as Piura and south to the giant border fortress of Paramonga (plate 118) on the central coast. This fortress, impregnable in its time, was flanked when the expanding Incas under Topa Inca Yupanqui, heir to the supreme power, assailed the Chimu Empire from the north and bypassed this southern border post during the reign (1438–71) of his father, Pachacuti Inca Yupanqui. True to the traditions of the coast, Paramonga was constructed of sun-dried adobe brick, quite in contrast to the later Inca fortification of Sacsahuamán (plates 116, 117), built of carefully worked blocks of stone in the highlands tradition.

Sacsahuamán overlooked Cuzco. Both Paramonga and Sacsahuamán reveal the warlike nature of much Andean Pre-Columbian history and give some idea of the height military architecture had reached as a consequence. Paramonga, with projecting corner bastions flanking otherwise exposed sections of planar wall, is comparable to the military architecture of Italy in the late fifteenth or sixteenth century. The successive walls and

46

terraces are arranged so that, as the bastions protect the walls, the upper terraces protect the lower ones. At Sacsahuamán, on the other hand, there is no flat curtain wall, but instead a construction *en tenaille*, in plan like the teeth of a saw, making a complex pattern of protection for the defenders. Like Paramonga, this fortress has a series of superimposed terraces so that the upper levels cover the ones below. As military architecture it is so advanced as to suggest French work of the seventeenth or eighteenth centuries.

Sacsahuamán and Cuzco itself (plates 109, 110) are standing testimonials to Inca stoneworking. Large stones of irregular shape are set in a matrix of somewhat smaller stones fitting as closely as the ground-glass stopper of a bottle. The parallel is apt, since the individual stones of a finely wrought Inca wall were set without mortar and actually ground into place.

One of the most spectacular of all Inca sites is Machu Picchu (plates 111–113), which lies on a saddle between two mountain peaks, 3000 feet above the Urubamba River, which winds around its base. Built of native rock, the buildings seem to grow from the geographical setting on a plan like a "patterned blanket thrown over a great rock," as Kubler has said.[60] Gable ends of houses echo the forms of the surrounding peaks, and terraces hold precious soil for gardens. Domestic architecture has trapezoidal doorways and niches cut into interior walls, diagnostic of Inca architecture, and walls are fitted onto projections of the living rock.

The architecture of the Incas uses a stark aesthetic of stone masonry, to the exclusion of the polychromy we have seen in Mexico or the sculptured relief patterns of Chanchan. Stones of irregular shape and size were mixed to create lively patterns, with surfaces sometimes emphasizing the shapes of the individual stones like the rustication of European architecture. Each stone either bulges slightly like a flattened pillow (plate 117) or is absorbed into the plane of the wall, probably by being ground on the outer surface in the same manner as the joints were ground to a high point of precision (plate 110). Another mode of building had the stones, as in the European tradition, set in horizontal beds that decrease in thickness as the wall rises, giving the effect of greater lightness above and stronger support below.

Cuzco, the Sacred City of the Incas, also followed the Inca pattern repeated consistently throughout their expanding do-

47

mains. It was laid out on a plan focusing on a main plaza with principal roads leading from this center; on a nearby height stood a protecting citadel—Sacsahuamán in the case of Cuzco. The main streets, once they left the city, became part of the extensive system of roads that made up the Capac Ñan, the Royal Highway of the Incas. Along its length were distributed at regular intervals *tampas*, or inns, for official travelers and messengers. Hanging bridges suspended from cables crossed rivers in mountain gorges (plate 122); staircases mounted to cross mountain ridges; and the highway was outlined with low protective walls when it crossed deserts of shifting sands.[61]

Inca architecture remains as the basis for present-day Cuzco. The Church of Santo Domingo rises over the foundations of the Inca Temple of the Sun (plate 109), and this juxtaposition shows us quite clearly the superiority of the Stone Age masonry of the Incas over the Iron Age masonry introduced by Spain. The changes wrought by the Old World in the New were not in all ways advances over native traditions and techniques.

48

For the convenience of the reader, each section of plates, 5–102 for Mexico and 103–122 for the Andes, is arranged alphabetically by site.

1. *Codex Nuttall, page 2, detail lower left. British Museum, London.*

Codex Mendoza, folio 10r. Bodleian Library, Oxford.

3. Mapa de Quinatzin, tracing (lower half). Bibliothèque Nationale, Paris.

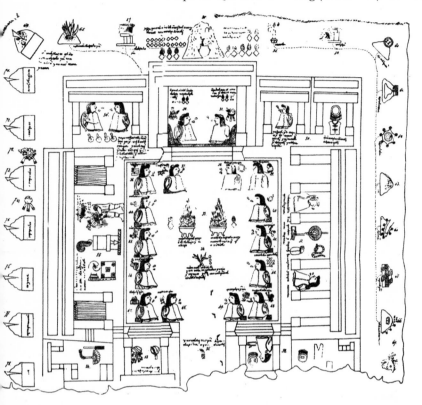

4. Codex Magliabecchiano, folio 69v. Biblioteca Nazionale Centrale, Florence.

5. *Round Pyramid of Quetzalcoatl, Calixtlahuaca.*

6. *Plaza of Pyramid of Tlaloc and cruciform altar, Calixtlahuaca.*

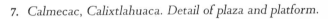

7. *Calmecac, Calixtlahuaca. Detail of plaza and platform.*

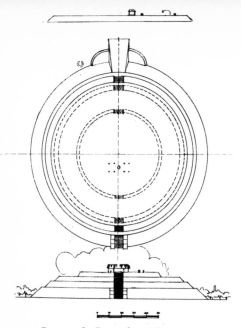

8. *Pyramid, Cuicuilco. Plan and elevation.*

9. *Pyramid, Cuicuilco.*

10. *Pyramid of the Niches, El Tajín. Plan.*

11. *Pyramid of the Niches, El Tajín.*

12. *Rock-cut temple, Malinalco.*

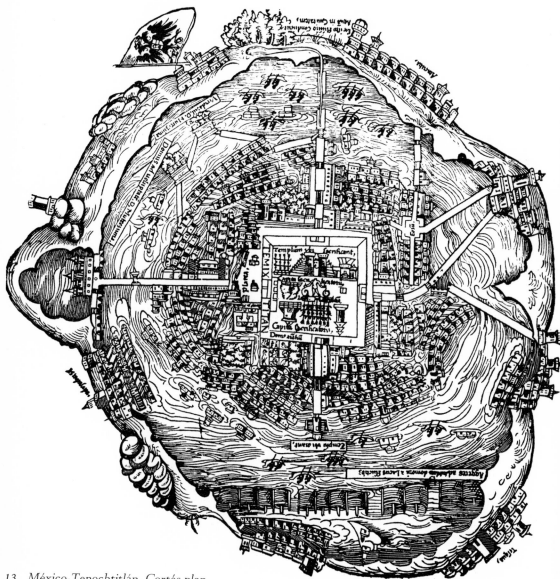

13. *México-Tenochtitlán. Cortés plan.*

4. Diego Rivera, "Market of Tlatelolco," fresco. Detail showing reconstruction of México-Tenochtitlán.

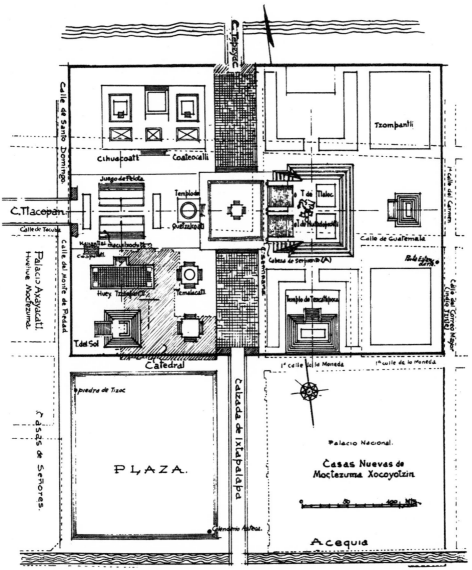

15. México-Tenochtitlán. Plan of principal plaza.

16. Mitla. Palace plans.

17. Building of the Columns, Mitla. Exterior façade.

18. Palace, Mitla. Detail of inner court.

19. Palace, Mitla. Detail of stone mosaic.

20. *Monte Albán. Site from South Platform.*

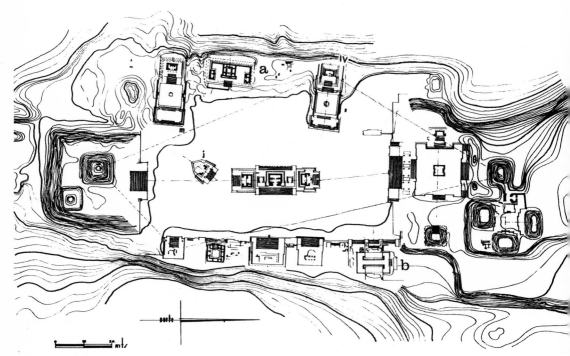

21. *Monte Albán. Site plan. a. Danzantes. b. Ball court. j. Observatory.*

22. *System IV and stele, Monte Albán.*

23. *Danzante, Monte Albán.*

24. *Observatory, Monte Albán. View from the rear.*

25. *Monte Albán. View of North Platform and colonnade from across sunken plaza.*

26. *Ball court, Monte Albán.*

27. Pyramid, Tenayuca. *Detail of Xiuhcóatl and coatepantli, or snake wall, seen from above.*

28. Pyramid, Tenayuca. *Detail showing lower stage of pyramid and* coatepantli.

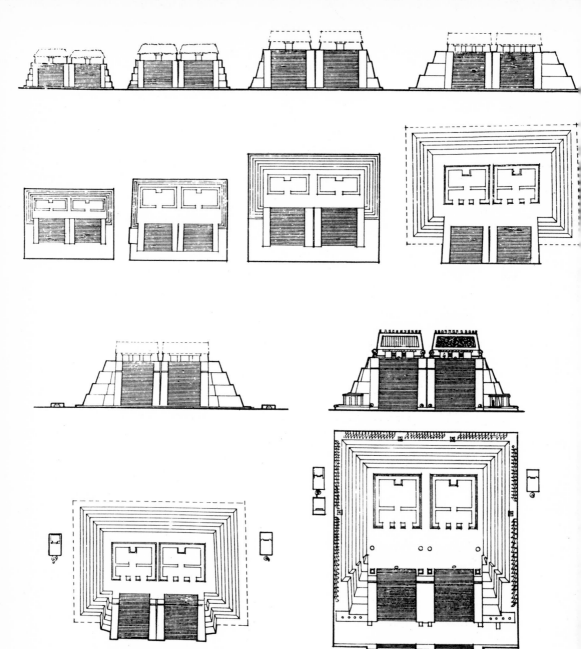

29. Pyramid, Tenayuca. Plans and elevations.

30. Pyramid, Tenayuca. Detail of staircase.

31. *Pyramid and temples, Teopanzalco.*

32. *Maison Carrée, Nîmes.*

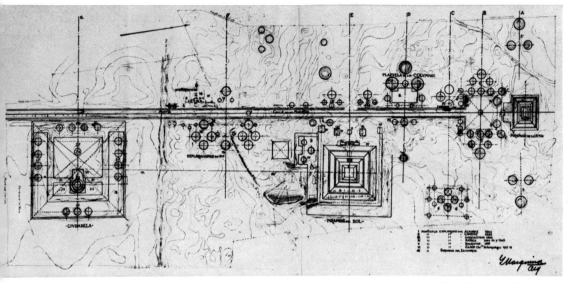

33. *Teotihuacán. Site plan.*

34. *Pyramid of the Sun, Teotihuacán.*

35. Pyramid of the Sun, Teotihuacán.

36. Citadel, Teotihuacán. Aerial view.

37. *Citadel, Teotihuacán. Detail of later addition to Pyramid of Quetzalcoatl.*

38. *Citadel, Teotihuacán. Pyramid of Quetzalcoatl from top of later addition.*

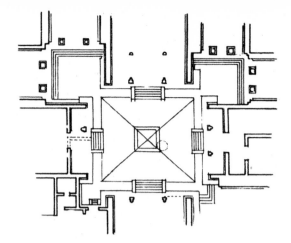

39. Atetelco, Teotihuacán. Plan of palace.

40. Atetelco, Teotihuacán. Palace patio with open corners.

41. Atetelco, Teotihuacán. Palace patio showing columns in antis and restoration of frescoes.

42. Atetelco, Teotihuacán. Mural, frieze of animals on the talud.

43. *Tula. General view of site.*

44. *Pyramid and Temple of Tlahuizcalpantecuhtli (Pyramid B) from Temple A, colonnade and plaza, Tula*

45. Pyramid of Tlahuizcalpantecuhtli, Tula. Detail of taluds and tableros, *lower stages*.

46. Pyramid of Tlahuizcalpantecuhtli, Tula. Detail of taluds and tableros.

47. *Temple of Tlahuizcalpantecuhtli, Tula. Telemones in place on pyramid.*

49. *Temple of Tlahuizcalpantecuhtli, Tula. Square column.*

48. *Temple of Tlahuizcalpantecuht Tula. Telemones.*

50. *Pyramid A, colonnade and plaza, Tula.* View from top of Pyramid of Tlahuizcalpantecuhtli.

51. *Palace, Tula.* View from Pyramid of Tlahuizcalpantecuhtli showing reconstructed colonnade.

52. *Temple, Xochicalco. Sculptural detail* on *talud* and *tablero.*

53. *A Maya building, Yucatán. Transverse section.*

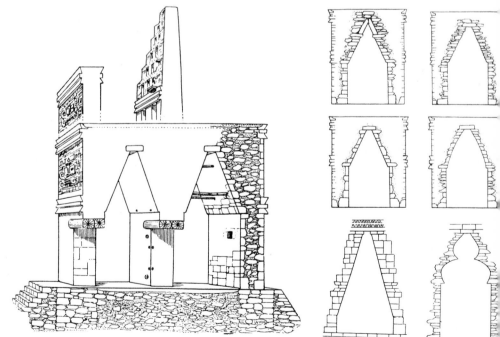

54. *Maya vaults. Sections*

55. "Preparation for a Dance," Detail of fresco. Structure 1, Room 1, Bonampak.

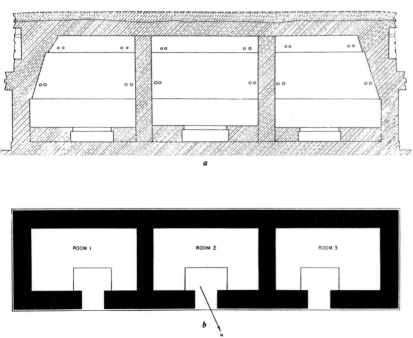

6. Palace, Bonampak. Palace of the Murals. a. Longitudinal cross section. b. Plan.

57. Chichén Itzá. Drawing of site.

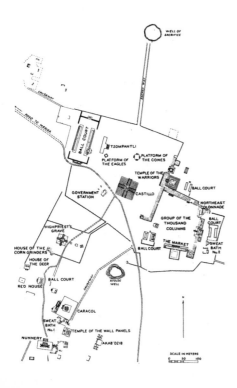

58. Chichén Itzá. Site plan, central section.

59. *The Castillo, Chichén Itzá.*

60. *The Castillo, Chichén Itzá. Plan.*

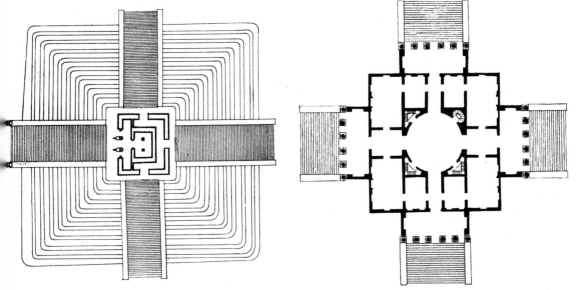

61. *Andrea Palladio. Villa Rotunda, Vicenza. Plan.*

62. Temple and Pyramid of the Warriors with colonnade, Chichén Itzá.

63. Temple of the Warriors and serpent columns, Chichén Itzá.

64. *The Caracol, Chichén Itzá.*

65. *Venus Platform, Chichén Itzá.*

66. *Chacmol, Chichén Itzá.*

67. *Telemon, Chichén Itzá.*

68. *Hieroglyphic Staircase, Copán. Detail figure. Peabody Museum, Harvard University.*

69. *Hieroglyphic Staircase. Structure 26, Copán.*

70. *Temple 22, Copán. Sculpture ornamenting doorway.*

71. *Limestone Maize God from Copán. American Museum of Natural History, New York.*

72. *Stele N, Copán. Engraving by Catherwood.*

73. *Principal building, Hochob. Model. Brooklyn Museum, New York.*

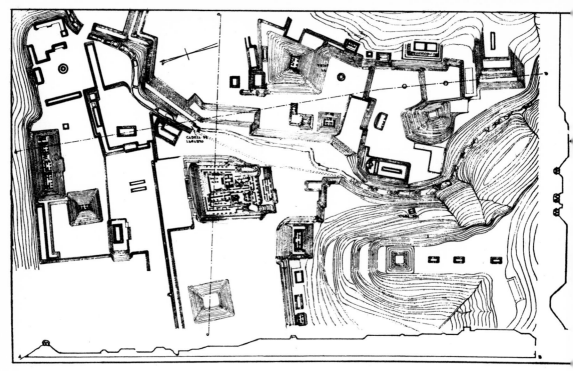

74. *Palenque. Site plan.*

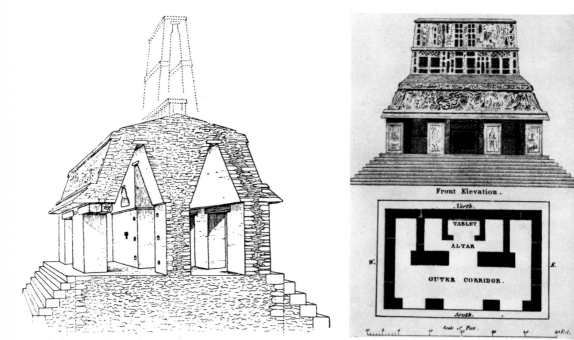

75. *Palenque. Typical cross section of a building.*

76. *Temple of the Cross, Palenque. Plan and elevation.*

77. *The Palace, Palenque. Stucco interior, House E.*

78. *The Palace, Palenque. Detail of stucco ornament, Pier F, House D.*

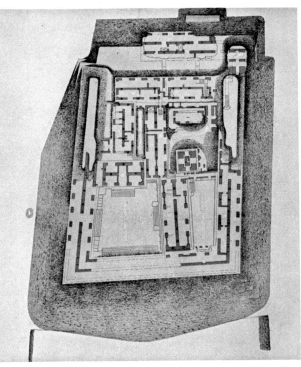

79. *The Palace, Palenque. Plan.*

The Palace and Tower, Palenque.

82. *Stele 12, Piedras Negras. University Museum, Philadelphia.*

81. *Acropolis, Piedras Negras.*

83. *Building 1, Río Bec. Model. American Museum of Natural History, New York.*

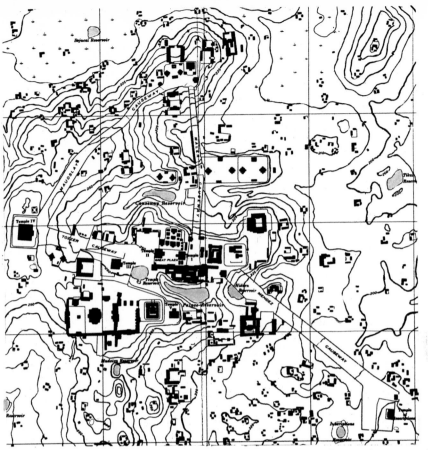

84. *Tikal. Site plan, central section.*

85. *Temple I (Temple of the Giant Jaguar), Tikal. During reconstruction.*

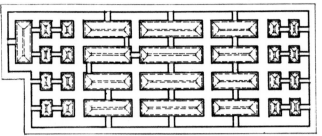

7. *Temples I and II, Tikal. a. Elevations. b. Cross sections. c. Plans.*

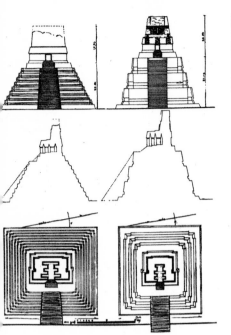

88. *Structure 51, South Acropolis, Tikal. Palace plan.*

89. *Maler's Palace, Tikal. Exterior.*

Palace of Five Stories, Tikal. Interior.

91. Tulum. Site plan.

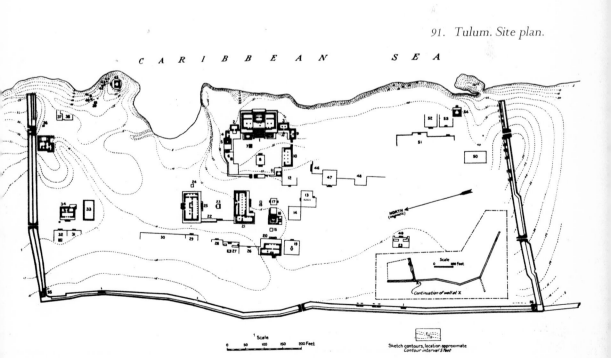

C A R I B B E A N   S E A

Scale
0   50   100   150   200 Feet

Sketch contours, location approximate
Contour interval 5 feet

92. *Pyramid E VII Sub, Uaxactún.*

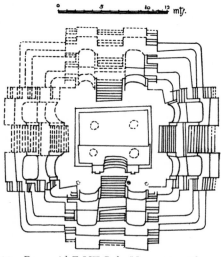

93. *Pyramid E VII Sub, Uaxactún. Plan.*

4. Michelangelo. Staircase of the Laurentian Library, Florence.

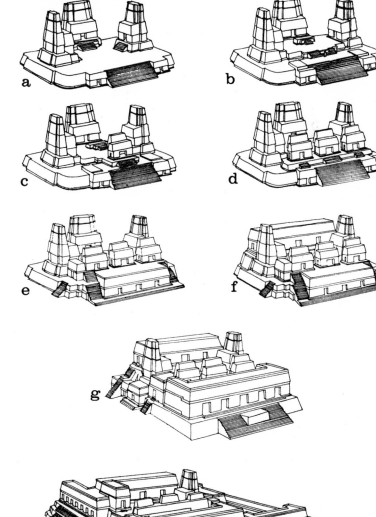

95. *Structure A-V, Temple-Palace complex, Uaxactún. a. First stage. b. Second stage. c. Third stage. d. Fourth stage. e. Fifth stage. f. Sixth stage. g. Seventh stage. h. Eighth stage.*

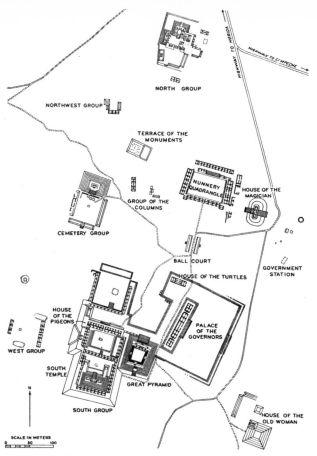

Labels on the site plan:

HIGHWAY TO MERIDA
HIGHWAY TO CAMPECHE

NORTH GROUP

NORTHWEST GROUP

TERRACE OF THE MONUMENTS

NUNNERY QUADRANGLE

HOUSE OF THE MAGICIAN

GROUP OF THE COLUMNS

CEMETERY GROUP

GOVERNMENT STATION

BALL COURT

HOUSE OF THE TURTLES

HOUSE OF THE PIGEONS

PALACE OF THE GOVERNORS

WEST GROUP

SOUTH TEMPLE

GREAT PYRAMID

N

SOUTH GROUP

HOUSE OF THE OLD WOMAN

SCALE IN METERS
0   50   100

96. Uxmal. Site plan, central section.

97. House of the Magician, Uxmal.

98. House of the Magician, Uxmal. Detail showing masks flanking staircase.

99. Nunnery, Uxmal. View into quadrangle showing façade of west wing from House of the Magician.

0. Nunnery, Uxmal. Detail of frieze, east wing.

101. Nunnery, Uxmal. Detail of house motif, south wing.

102. Palace of the Governors, Uxmal.

103. Compounds, Chanchan. Aerial view.

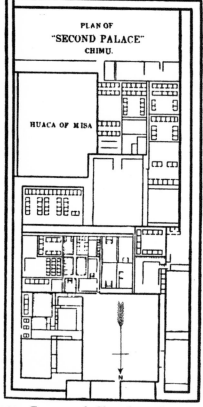

104. Compound, Chanchan. Plan.

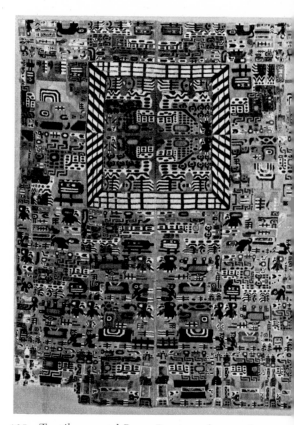

105. Textile, coastal Peru. Portion of a poncho.
Bliss Collection, Washington, D.C.

106. Hall of the Arabesques, Chanchan. View of mud relief.

107. Textile, coastal Peru. Portion of a mantle (?). Bliss Collection, Washington, D.C.

108. Chavín de Huántar, lanzón in the Castillo.

110. Cuzco. Street showing Inca masonry.
(Photo: courtesy Grace Line)

109. Cuzco. Inca Temple of the Sun as the base of the Church of Santo Domingo.

1. *Inca buildings, Machu Picchu.*

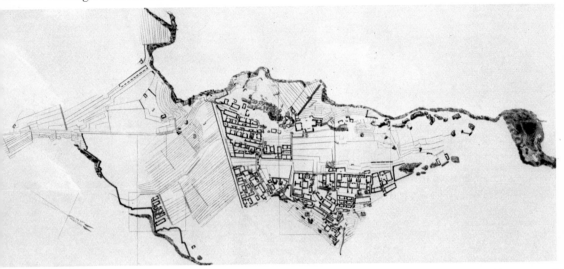

112. *Machu Picchu. Site plan.*

113. *Inca masonry, Machu Picchu.*

114. *Temple of the Sun, Moche. Detail showing masonry.*

115. *Mochica House, model ceramic jar.*

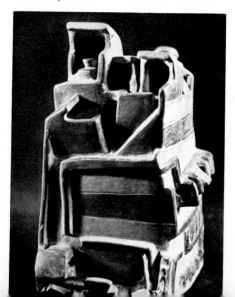

116. *Masonry fortifications, Sacsahuamán. (Photo: courtesy of Grace Line)*

117. *Masonry fortifications, Sacsahuamán. Detail of stone wall.*

118. Fortress of adobe brick, Paramonga. Aerial view.

119. *Gate of the Sun, Tiahuanaco. (Photo: courtesy of Grace Line)*

121. *Textile, coast Tiahuanaco. Miniature shirt.*
Brooklyn Museum, New York.

20. *Gate of the Sun, Tiahuanaco. Central figure.*

122. *Inca bridge over the Apurimac River.*

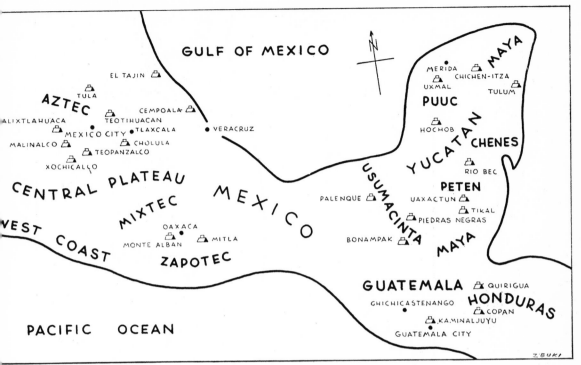

Map A. Mexico

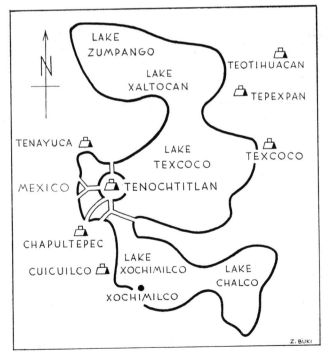

Map B. Valley of Mexico

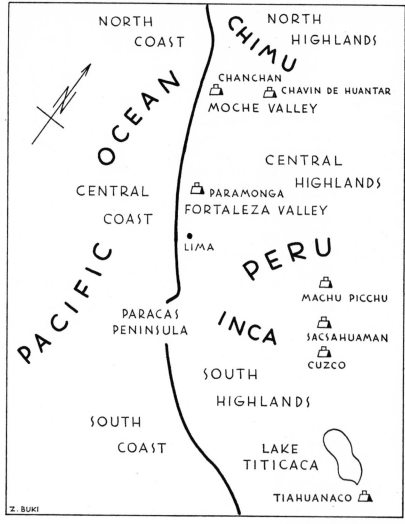

Map C. The Andes

CHRONOLOGICAL CHART

MIDDLE AMERICA

APPROXIMATE DATES	PERIOD	CENTRAL MEXICO	PERIPHERAL MEXICO	MAYA AREA
12,000–8000 B.C.	Pre-Formative	Ixtapan site Tepexpán Man		
1500 B.C.–100 A.D.	Formative or Pre-Classic	Cuicuilco		Uaxactún (E VII Sub)
100–900 A.D.	Classic	Teotihuacan	Cholula El Tajín Kaminaljuyú (Guatemala) Monte Albán Xochicalco	Bonampak Copán Hochob Palenque Piedras Negras Río Bec Tikal Uaxactún Uxmal Xpuhil
900–1519/1521 A.D.	Post-Classic	México-Tenoch-titlán Tenayuca Tlatelolco Tula	Calixtlahuaca Malinalco Mitla Teopanzalco Tizatlán	Chichén Itzá Mayapán Tulum
1519–1521 A.D.	Spanish Conquest			

CHRONOLOGICAL CHART

APPROXIMATE DATES	PERIOD	SITES	AREA
3000–1000 B.C.	Early Farmer		
1000–1 B.C.	Cultist	Chavín de Huántar	north highlands
1–600 A.D.	Experimenter		
600–1000 A.D.	Master Craftsman	Moche	north coast
1000–1200 A.D.	Expansionist	Tiahuanaco	south highlands
1200–1450 A.D.	City Builder	Chanchan Paramonga	north coast central coast
1450–1532 A.D.	Imperialist (Inca)	Cuzco Machu Picchu Sacsahuamán	central highlands central highlands central highlands
1532 A.D.	Spanish Conquest		

Parallels between the Andean region and Middle America are not direct, but the following can be suggested: Imperialist Inca–the Aztecs of México-Tenochtitlán; City Builder Chanchan–Tula; Expansionist Tiahuanaco–Teotihuacán; Cultist Chavín de Huántar–Cuicuilco; Early Farmer–Pre-Formative.

NOTES

1. Still the best account of the Conquest of Mexico is William H. Prescott, *History of the Conquest of Mexico...*, New York, Modern Library, n.d.
2. See the discussion of the plan, p. 39 and note 48 *infra*.
3. Henry B. Nicholson, "Montezuma's Zoo," *Pacific Discovery*, VIII, No. 4, July-August, 1955, pp. 3–11. Other important types of buildings in Middle America include: astronomical observatories (plate 24), sweat baths, and markets. Other works suggesting architecture but closer to engineering were: viaducts, reservoirs, and fortifications. For an extended discussion of certain of these types, see the section on City Plans.
4. Bernal Díaz del Castillo, *The Discovery and Conquest of Mexico, 1517–1521*, Introduction by Irving A. Leonard, New York, 1956, pp. 190–91.
5. George A. Kubler, *Mexican Architecture of the Sixteenth Century*, New Haven, 1948, I, pp. 71–72, 76.
6. Hereinafter referred to as México-Tenochtitlán when the Pre-Columbian city is meant. The present capital of the Republic of Mexico will be referred to as Mexico City, and the area occupied by the present Republic of Mexico, excluding the peninsula of Yucatán and other areas of Maya-speaking occupation, will be called Mexico. Middle America includes Mexico and the Maya area.
7. Díaz del Castillo, *op. cit.*; Hernando Cortés, *Letters of Cortés*, trans. by F. A. Mac-Nutt, 2 vols., New York and London, 1908; Anonymous Conqueror, *Narrative of Some Things of New Spain*, ed. and trans. by Marshall H. Saville, New York, The Cortés Society, 1917.
8. The interesting study of Robert H. Barlow, *The Extent of the Empire of the Culhua Mexica*, Ibero-Americana, 28, Berkeley and Los Angeles, 1949, discusses the problem of nomenclature and gives much information on the tribute rendered the Triple Alliance.
9. *Ibid.*
10. George Clapp Vaillant, *Aztecs of Mexico: Origin, Rise and Fall of the Aztec Nation*, Garden City, New York, 1947, p. 84 and *passim*.
11. Vaillant, *op. cit.* See also Alfonso Caso, *La Religión de los Aztecas*, Mexico, 1936, and his more recent version, *El Pueblo del Sol*, Mexico, 1953.
12. The round Pyramid of Quetzalcoatl as Ehécatl at Calixtlahuaca (plate 5) is an example. Iconography as a rule enters architecture through architectural sculpture and painting rather than architectural form as such.
13. Vaillant, *op. cit.*, pp. 81–82.
14. Central Mexico includes those sites in the central Valley of Mexico and nearby, e.g., Tula and Teotihuacán. Peripheral Mexico refers to all other sites in Mexico excluding the Maya area. Nahuatl, the language of the Aztecs, dominated the central Valley of Mexico; Otomi was spoken to the north, Tarascan to the west, Mixtec and Zapotec to the south in the vicinity of Oaxaca city, while outside central and peripheral Mexico, Maya dialects prevailed. The Nahuatl and Maya languages are still in use.
15. See Román Piña Chán, *Las Culturas preclásicas de la Cuenca de México*, Mexico, 1955.
16. Donald Robertson, *Mexican Manuscript Painting of the Early Colonial Period: The Metropolitan Schools*, Yale Historical Publications, History of Art 12, New Haven, 1959, discusses the manuscript sources of Mexican pre-Conquest history. Tula derives instead from Chichén Itzá according to a recent unorthodox article; see George Kubler, "Chichén Itzá y Tula," *Estudios de cultura maya*, 1, Mexico, 1961, pp. 47–79.

17. See plate 101 for a native thatched-roof house used as a decorative motif on the nunnery at Uxmal.

18. Sub-pyramid burial is found in Middle America, but the pyramid is essentially a platform supporting a temple, and the burial is ancillary rather than primary.

19. Prescott, *op. cit.*, pp. 335–36, gives us a vivid description of the interior of the Aztec temple, and Díaz del Castillo, *op. cit.*, pp. 219–20, provides an eyewitness account.

20. The true arch was not known in the New World.

21. Subsequent round temples include those of Calixtlahuaca (plate 5) and Malinalco (plate 12).

22. Charles E. Dibble, *Códice Xolotl*, Publicaciones del Instituto de Historia, Ser. 1, 22, Mexico, 1951.

23. A recent study from Teotihuacán, although somewhat unorthodox, is Laurette Séjourné, *Un Palacio en la ciudad de los dioses* [*Teotihuacán*], Mexico, 1959. Continuing studies of René Millon promise exciting discoveries in the future; see articles in *American Antiquity*, XXVI, 1959–1960.

24. The first gathering of information on the location of Tula and a study of the sources was Wigberto Jiménez Moreno, "Tula y los Toltecas según las fuentes históricas," *Revista mexicana de estudios anthropológicos*, V, No. 2–3, Mexico, May–Dec., 1941, pp. 79–83.

25. A name given to the pyramid in recent times, it is the name of a god in the Aztec pantheon meaning Lord of the House of Dawn. He was associated with Venus as the morning star and a variant aspect of Quetzalcoatl.

26. See also the Temple of Xochicalco (plate 52) to the south for the sculptural treatment of the *tableros* and *taluds*; in central and peripheral Mexico temple walls as well as pyramid facings received this *tablero-talud* treatment. The Náhuatl word for this covering was *tzaqualli*, meaning covered with a revetment.

27. In a recent publication Marquina has described a model of the main temple and its subsidiary buildings now on display in the Museo Etnográfico of Mexico City. See Ignacio Marquina, *El Templo mayor de México*, Mexico, 1960.

28. Another similar pyramid has been discovered at Acanceh. See also the Castillo, Chichén Itzá (plates 59, 60), for a later development of this plan.

29. For a fine publication of a Teotihuacán palace, see Séjourné, *op. cit.*

30. See Karl Ruppert, *The Mercado, Chichén Itzá, Yucatán*, Carnegie Institution of Washington, Publication 546, Contributions to American Anthropology and History, VIII, No. 43, Washington, D.C., 1943. The building at Calixtlahuaca known as the *calmecac* (plate 7), or priestly school, preserves an even simpler type, where many small rooms and little courts are given formal importance merely by the raised platform they stand on, fronting a large plaza which seems almost to function as an external patio for the group.

31. In plate 15 the site of Montezuma's palace is labeled "Casas Nuevas de Moctezuma Xocoyotzin." The outline of the present National Palace is shown with a broken line. The model of Marquina (see note 27, *supra*) shows Aztec-period-"palace-type" buildings, including the *calmecac*, or priestly school, of México-Tenochtitlán, within the sacred enclosure. For an excavated Aztec palace, see Alfred M. Tozzer, *Excavation of a Site at Santiago Ahuitzotla, D. F., Mexico*, Bureau of American Ethnology, Bulletin 74, Washington, D.C., 1921; at this site, unfortunately, only a series of superimposed foundation walls remain.

32. Tatiana Proskouriakoff, *An Album of Maya Architecture*, Carnegie Institution of Washington, Publication 558, Washington, D.C., 1946, 28–35.

33. The spiral staircase of the Caracol at Chichén Itzá (plate 64), dating from the Mexican period of the Maya, is another example of a complicated staircase.

34. Carved stone skulls dotting the cruciform altar at Calixtlahuaca (plate 6) were probably also covered with stucco and painted.

35. See Miguel Covarrubias, *Indian Art of Mexico and Central America*, New York, 1957, Chapter 11, "The Olmec Problem," pp. 50–83. Formal relations, at least, with the fresco of the "Earthly Paradise" at Tepantitla, Teotihuacán, in the Classic period should also be investigated.

36. Alfonso Caso, *Las Estelas zapotecas*, Mexico, 1928, gives the most complete catalogue of the sculptured steles at Monte Albán.

37. See Tatiana Proskouriakoff, *A Study of Classic Maya Sculpture*, Carnegie Institution of Washington, Publication 593, Washington, D.C., 1950.

38. John Lloyd Stephens, *Incidents of Travel in Central America, Chiapas and Yucatan*, drawings by F. Catherwood, 2 vols., New York, 1841.

39. Alfred Percival Maudslay, *Biologia Centrali-Americana*, Vol. 4, *Archaeology (Palenque)*, London, 1896–99.

40. Alfonso Caso, "Las Ruinas de Tizatlán, Tlaxcala," *Revista mexicana de estudios históricos*, I, No. 4, Mexico, 1927, pp. 139–72.

41. In the present careful reconstruction the painting has a border which outlines the doorway and the joinings of wall to wall and walls to ceiling, further supporting and strengthening the architectural layout.

42. The Teotihuacán frescoes are sometimes monochromatic, and the principle, of course, still holds.

43. The southern end of the Miccaotli does not seem to have been established. The recent work of Millon (see note 23 *supra*) indicates the city is larger than originally thought, and leads one to believe that excavations at the south end would cast new light on its extent in that direction.

44. Millon's work has put the dating at Teotihuacán into question. For instance, the pyramids of the Sun and of the Moon seem to be among the earliest buildings at the site, but the subordinate buildings may be later.

45. George Kubler, "The Design of Space in Maya Architecture," *Miscellanea Paul Rivet*, *octogenario dicata*, XXXI International Congress of Americanists, Mexico, 1958, I, pp. 515–31.

46. Note the cruciform altar at Calixtlahuaca (plate 6) as a post-Classic example of the obelisk effect even though it is not radially symmetrical.

47. Alfonso Caso, "Los Barrios antiguos de Tenochtitlán y Tlatelolco," *Memorias de la Academia mexicana de la Historia*, XV, No. 1, Mexico, 1956, pp. 7–63; Manuel Toussaint, Federico Gómez de Orozco, and Justino Fernández, *Planos de la ciudad de México, siglos XVI y XVII*, Mexico, 1938.

48. The controversy over the plan of México-Tenochtitlán is discussed in Kubler, *Mexican Architecture*, I, p. 74; a more recent marshaling of evidence on the plan appears in Robertson, *op. cit.*, pp. 77–83; the older view is presented in Dan Stanislawski, "The Origin and Spread of the Grid-pattern Town," *The Geographical Review*, XXXVI, No. 1, New York, 1946, pp. 105–20.

49. For a discussion of the date of this manuscript plan of a part of México-Tenochtitlán, see Robertson, *op. cit.*, pp. 77–83.

50. An unpublished thesis of Willard Sloshberg of the Tulane Graduate School suggests the defensive arrangement of buildings around sunken plazas in the Maya area. See also J. Eric S. Thompson, *The Rise and Fall of Maya Civilization*, Norman, Oklahoma, 1954, pp. 105–07.

51. Inca was the title of the ruler of the people commonly called the Incas. The word will be used interchangeably for both the ruler and his people.

52. The most convenient additional source of information on Inca society is J. Alden Mason, *The Ancient Civilizations of Peru*, Pelican (A395), Harmondsworth and Baltimore, 1957.

53. For a significant study of Andean textiles, see Cora Elder Stafford, *Paracas Embroideries*, New York, 1941.

54. For Andean history, see Mason, *op. cit.*, and Wendell C. Bennett and Junius B. Bird,

Andean Culture History, American Museum of Natural History, Handbook Series No. 15, New York, 1949.

55. Philip Ainsworth Means, *Fall of the Inca Empire and the Spanish Rule in Peru: 1530–1780*, New York and London, 1932. The native culture had no highly developed system of writing like the Mexican and Maya hieroglyphs, although some information could be conveyed by the *quipu*, a device of knotted and colored cords. We do not know how much more than a merely mnemonic aid it was.

56. Hermann Leicht, *Pre-Inca Art and Culture*, New York, 1960.

57. No plan of this important but inadequately studied building has been published. See Hans-Dietrich Disselhoff and Sigvald Linné, *The Art of Ancient America, Civilizations of Central and South America*, New York, 1960, pp. 158 and 161.

58. George Kubler, "Los Pueblos clásicos mochica," *Anales del Instituto de Arte Americano e Investigaciones Estéticas*, XII, Buenos Aires, 1959, pp. 9–23.

59. A comparison of plates 103, 104 and 105 points out suggestive similarities between textile patterns and the plans of Chanchan buildings, both constructed in a system dominated by verticals and horizontals which hold the individual units fast.

60. George Kubler, "Machu Picchu," *Perspecta, the Yale Architectural Journal*, VI, New Haven, 1960, pp. 48–55, p. 53.

61. A recent study of the Inca roads sums up what was previously known and adds new material from studies of an expedition that traced their course. See Victor Wolfgang Von Hagen, *Highway of the Sun*, New York, 1955.

SELECTED BIBLIOGRAPHY

References given in notes are not repeated here. The following abbreviations are used:
 CIW – Carnegie Institution of Washington
 INAH–OG – Instituto Nacional de Antropología e Historia, Mexico – Official Guide

MIDDLE AMERICA: *General*

Archeology in Mexico Today, Mexico, Petroleos Mexicanos, n.d.

Brainerd, G. W., *The Maya Civilization*, Los Angeles, 1954.

Esplendor del México antiguo, Centro de Investigaciones Antropológicas de México, 2 vols., Mexico, 1959.

Handbook of Middle American Indians, Robert Wauchope, ed. (in preparation).

Holmes, William H., *Archaeological Studies Among the Ancient Cities of Mexico*, Field Columbian Museum, Anthropological Series, I, No. 1, Chicago, 1895–97.

Kelemen, Pál, *Medieval American Art*, 2 vols., New York, 1956.

Krickeberg, Walter, *Altmexikanische Kulturen*, Berlin, 1956.

Kubler, George, *Art and Architecture of Ancient America* (Pelican History of Art), Penguin, 1962.

Landa's Relación de las cosas de Yucatán, trans. and ed. by Alfred M. Tozzer, Papers of the Peabody Museum of American Archaeology and Ethnology, Harvard University, XVIII, Cambridge, Mass., 1941.

Marquina, Ignacio, *Arquitectura prehispánica*, Memorias del Institutio Nacional de Antropología e Historia, I, Mexico, 1951.

México prehispánico, Emma Hurtado, ed., Mexico, 1946.

Morley, Sylvanus Griswold, *The Ancient Maya*, Stanford University, 1947.

——, *The Ancient Maya*, 3d ed., rev. by George W. Brainerd, Stanford University, 1956.

Peterson, Frederick A., *Ancient Mexico*, New York, 1959.

Spinden, Herbert J., *Maya Art and Civilization*, Indian Hills, Colorado, 1957.

Stephens, John Lloyd, *Incidents of Travel in Central America*, 2 vols., New Brunswick, 1949.

——, *Incidents of Travel in Yucatan*, Victor Wolfgang Von Hagen, ed., 2 vols., Norman, Oklahoma, 1960.

Thompson, J. Eric S., *The Civilization of the Mayas*, Field Museum of Natural History, Anthropology Leaflet 25, 2d ed., Chicago, 1932.

——, *Mexico Before Cortez, an Account of the Daily Life, Religion and Ritual of the Aztecs and Kindred Peoples*, New York and London, 1933.

Toscano, Salvador, *Arte precolombino de México y de la América Central*, Mexico, 1944.

Vaillant, George C., *The Aztecs of Mexico*, Penguin (A 200), Baltimore, 1960.

Von Hagen, Victor Wolfgang, *The Aztec: Man and Tribe*, Mentor (MD 236), New York, 1958.

——, *World of the Maya*, Mentor (MD 300), New York, 1960.

Westheim, Paul, *Arte antiguo de México*, 1950.

Wolf, Eric R., *Sons of the Shaking Earth*, Chicago, 1959.

MEXICO BY SITF

CALIXTLAHUACA ˙

García Payón, José, *La Zona arqueológica de Tecaxic-Calixtlahuaca y los Matlatzincas*, Mexico, 1936.

INAH–OG, 1960.

CUICUILCO:

INAH–OG, 1959 (with Copilco).

See also work cited in note 15, *supra*.

EL TAJÍN:

García Payón, José, *Exploraciones en El Tajín, temporadas 1953 y 1954*, Informes 2, Mexico, 1955.

INAH–OG, 1957.

MALINALCO:

García Payón, José, "Los Monumentos arqueológicos de Malinalco, Estado de México," *Revista mexicana de estudios antropológicos*, VIII, Nos. 1–3, Mexico, 1946, pp. 5–63.

INAH–OG, 1958.

MÉXICO-TENOCHTITLÁN:

INAH–OG, 1957 *(Templo mayor de México)*

See also works cited in notes 3, 27, and 47–49, *supra*.

MITLA:

Caso, Alfonso, and Rubín de la Borbolla, D. F., *Exploraciones en Mitla, 1934–1935*, Instituto Panamericano de Geografía e Historia 21, Mexico, 1936.

INAH–OG, 1957 (with Monte Albán)

MONTE ALBÁN:

Caso, Alfonso, *Exploraciones en Oaxaca, quinta y sexta temporadas 1936–1937*, Instituto Panamericano de Geografía e Historia 34, Tacubaya, D. F., 1938.

——, *Las Exploraciones en Monte Albán, temporada 1931–1932*, Institutio Panamericano de Geografía e Historia 7, Mexico, 1932.

INAH–OG, 1957 (with Mitla)

See also work cited in note 36, *supra*.

TENAYUCA:

Tenayuca, estudio arqueológico, Mexico, 1935.

INAH–OG, 1960.

TEOPANZALCO:

Ceballos Novelo, Roque J., *Ruinas arqueológicas de Tepoztlán y Teopanzalco, Estado de Morelos*, Mexico, 1933.

Zonas arqueológicos del Estado de Morelos, INAH–OG, 1960.

TEOTIHUACÁN:

Gamio, Manuel, ed., *La Población del Valle de Teotihuacán*, Mexico, 1922, t. 1, Vol. 1, Pt. 2.

Linné, Sigvald, *Archaeological Researches at Teotihuacán, Mexico*, The Ethnographical Museum of Sweden, new ser., Publication No. 1, Stockholm, 1934.

INAH–OG, 1956.

See also works cited in note 23, *supra*.

TLATELOLCO:

Tlatelolco a través de los tiempos (articles by various authors published in *Memorias de la Academia mexicana de la Historia*, Mexico, 1944–   ).

See also works cited in notes 47–49, *supra*.

TULA:

Caso, Alfonso, "El Complejo arqueológico de Tula y las grandes culturas indígenas de México," *Revista mexicana de estudios antropológicos*, V, Nos. 2–3, Mexico, May-Dec., 1941, pp. 85–95.

INAH–OG, 1957.

See also work cited in notes 16 and 24, *supra*.

XOCHICALCO:

Noguera, Eduardo, *Ruinas arqueológicas de Xochicalco, Morelos*, Mexico, 1929.

Zonas arqueológicos del Estado de Morelos, INAH-OG, 1960.

MAYA AREA BY SITE

Las ciudades mayas, INAH–OG, 1958.

BONAMPAK:

Ancient Maya Paintings of Bonampak, Mexico, CIW, Supplementary Publication 46, Washington, D.C., 1955.

Ruppert, Karl J., Thompson, Eric S., and Proskouriakoff, Tatiana, *Bonampak, Chiapas, Mexico* (copies of mural paintings by Antonio Tejeda; identification of pigments by Rutherford J. Gettens), CIW, Publication 602, Washington, D.C., 1955.

CHICHÉN ITZÁ:

Morris, Earl H., Charlot, Jean, and Morris, Ann Axtell, *The Temple of the Warriors at Chichén Itzá, Yucatan*, CIW, Publication 406, 2 vols., Washington, D.C., 1931.

Ruppert, Karl, *Chichen Itza: Architectural Notes and Plans*, CIW, Publication 595, Washington, D.C., 1952.

Tozzer, Alfred M., *Chichen Itza and Its Cenote of Sacrifice*, Memoirs of the Peabody Museum of Archaeology and Ethnology, Harvard University, XI, XII, Cambridge, Mass., 1957.

INAH–OG, 1958.

See also work cited in notes 16 and 30, *supra*.

COPÁN:

Gordon, George Byron, *The Hieroglyphic Stairway, Ruins of Copan; Report on Explorations by the Museum*, Memoirs of the Peabody Museum of Archaeology and Ethnology, Harvard University, I, No. 6, Cambridge, Mass., 1902.

Morley, Sylvanus Griswold, *The Inscriptions at Copan*, CIW, Publication 219, Washington, D.C., 1920.

PALENQUE:

Ruz Lhuillier, Alberto, "The Mystery of the Temple of the Inscriptions [at Palenque, Mexico]," trans. by J. Alden Mason, *Archaeology*, VI, No. 1, March, 1953, pp. 3–11.

INAH–OG, 1959.

See also work cited in note 39, *supra*.

PIEDRAS NEGRAS:

Satterthwaite, Linton, Jr., Piedras Negras articles (various) in publications of the University Museum, University of Pennsylvania, Philadelphia, 1930's and 1940's.

TIKAL:

Shook, Edwin M., various articles in *Expedition, the Bulletin of the University Museum of the University of Pennsylvania*, Philadelphia, 1958– .

———, and others, *Tikal Reports, Nos. 1–4*, Museum Monographs, Philadelphia, University Museum, University of Pennsylvania, 1958.

Tozzer, Alfred M., *A Preliminary Study of the Prehistoric Ruins of Tikal, Guatemala; a Report of the Peabody Museum Expedition, 1909–1910*, Memoirs of the Peabody Museum of Archaeology and Ethnology, Harvard University, V, No. 2, Cambridge, Mass., 1911.

TULUM:

Lothrop, Samuel K., *Tulum, an Archaeological Study of the East Coast of Yucatan*, CIW, Publication 335, Washington, D.C., 1924.

INAH–OG, 1959 (Spanish); 1961 (English)

UAXACTÚN:

Ricketson, Oliver G., Jr., and Ricketson, Edith Bayles, *Uaxactun, Guatemala, Group E, 1926–1931*, CIW, Publication 477, Washington, D.C., 1937.

Smith, A. Ledyard, *Uaxactun, Guatemala: Excavations of 1931–1937*, CIW, Publication 588, Washington, D.C., 1950.

UXMAL:

INAH–OG, 1959.

THE ANDES: *General*

The Andean Civilizations, Julian H. Steward, ed., Vol. II of *Handbook of South American Indians*, Smithsonian Institution, Bureau of American Ethnology, Bulletin 143, Washington, D.C., 1946.

Bennett, Wendell C., *A Reappraisal of Peruvian Archaeology*, Memoirs of the Society for American Archaeology, 4 (Supplement to *American Antiquity*, XIII, No. 4, Pt. 2), Salt Lake City, April, 1948.

———, *Ancient Arts of the Andes*, New York, Museum of Modern Art, 1954.

Bushnell, G. H. S., *Peru*, Ancient Peoples and Places, I, London, 1956.

Kelemen, Pál, *Medieval American Art*, 2 vols., New York, 1956.

Kroeber, A. L., *Archaeological Explorations in Peru*, Field Museum of Natural History, Anthropology Memoirs, II, Chicago, 1926–37.

———, "Art," in *The Comparative Ethnology of South American Indians*, Vol. V of *Handbook of South American Indians*, Smithsonian Institution, Bureau of American Ethnology, Bulletin 143, Washington, D.C., 1949, pp. 411–92.

Kubler, George, *Art and Architecture of Ancient America* (Pelican History of Art), Penguin, 1962.

Lehmann, Walter, with Doering, Heinrich, *The Art of Old Peru*, Berlin [1924].

Means, Philip Ainsworth, *Ancient Civilizations of the Andes*, New York, 1931.

Prescott, William H., *History of the Conquest of Mexico and History of the Conquest of Peru*, New York, Modern Library, n.d.

Squier, Ephraim George, *Peru Illustrated or, Incidents of Travel and Exploration in the Land of the Incas*, New York, 1877.

Tello, Julio C., "Andean Civilization: Some Problems of Peruvian Archaeology," *Proceedings of the Twenty-Third International Congress of Americanists Held at New York, September 17–22, 1928*, New York, 1930, pp. 259–90.

Thompson, J. Eric S., *Archaeology of South America*, Field Museum of Natural History, Anthropology Leaflet 33, Chicago, 1936.

Ubbelohde-Doering, Heinrich, *The Art of Ancient Peru*, New York, 1952.

Von Hagen, Victor Wolfgang, *Realm of the Incas*, Mentor (MD 192), New York, 1957.

THE ANDES BY SITE

CHAVÍN DE HUÁNTAR:

Tello, Julio C., *Chavin, cultura matriz de la civilización andina*, Lima, 1960.

———, "Discovery of the Chavín Culture in Peru," *American Antiquity*, IX, No. 1, July, 1943, pp. 135–60.

CUZCO:

Rowe, John H., *An Introduction to the Archaeology of Cuzco*, Papers of the Peabody Museum of American Archaeology and Ethnology, Harvard University, XXVII, No. 2, Cambridge, Mass., 1944.

MACHU PICCHU:

Bingham, Hiram, *Lost City of the Incas, the Story of Machu Picchu and Its Builders*, New York, 1948.

———, *Machu Picchu, A Citadel of the Incas, Report of the Explorations and Excavations Made in 1911, 1912, and 1915 Under the Auspices of Yale University and the National Geographic Society*, New Haven, 1930.

See also work cited in note 60, *supra*.

MOCHE:

See work cited in note 58, *supra*.

TIAHUANACO:

Posnansky, Arthur, *Tihuanacu, the Cradle of American Man*, 2 vols., New York, 1946.

VIRÚ VALLEY:

Willey, Gordon R., *Prehistoric Settlement Patterns in the Virú Valley*, Smithsonian Institution, Bureau of American Ethnology, Bulletin 155, Washington, D.C., 1953.

INDEX

Numbers in regular roman type refer to text pages; *italic* figures refer to the plates.

SOURCES OF ILLUSTRATIONS

Alinari-Anderson, Florence: 94

American Antiquity, IX, 1: 108

Courtesy of the American Museum of Natural History, New York: 71, 83, 86, 103

Anales del Museo Nacional de México, I (Mexico, 1886): 3

Anton, Ferdinand, Munich: 17, 18, 20, 23, 24, 26, 34, 59, 62, 63, 65, 66, 67, 80, 85, 97, 99, 100, 102

Barton, M., New Orleans:22

Bennett, Wendell C., *Ancient Art of the Andes* (New York, 1954). Photo: Pierre Verger: 117

Biblioteca Nazionale Centrale, Florence (Photo by G. B. Pineider): 4

The Robert Woods Bliss Collection, Washington, D.C. (Photos by Nickolas Muray): 105, 107

Courtesy Bodleian Library, Oxford: 2

Courtesy British Museum, London: 1

Courtesy Brooklyn Museum, New York: 73, 121

Buki, Zoltan F., Lafayette, Louisiana: maps pp. 113, 114

Burger, Fritz, *Die Villen des Andrea Palladio* (Leipzig, 1910): 61

Burnham, A. Dwight, Lawrence, Kan.: 19, 25

Carnegie Institution of Washington, Sup. Pub. 46, 1955: 55 (painting by Antonio Tejeda), 56

Fairchild Aerial Surveys, Inc., New York: 118

Fairchild from Compañía Mexicana: 36

Fondo Editorial de la Plástica Mexicana, *Mural Painting of the Mexican Revolution, 1921–1960* (Mexico, 1961): 14

French Government Tourist Office, New York: 32

Gamio, Manuel, ed., *La Población del Valle de Teotihuacán*, I, (Mexico, 1922): 33 (plan by Marquina)

Courtesy Grace Line, New York: 110, 116, 119

Foto A. Guillén M., Lima, Peru: 115

Holmes, William H., *Archaeological Studies Among the Ancient Cities of Mexico*, Field Columbian Museum, Anthropological Series, I, 1 (Chicago, 1895–97): 16, 53, 54, 75.

Holton, George, Photo Library, Inc., New York: 111

Kubler, George, New Haven: 114

Lehmann, Walter, with Doering, Heinrich, *The Art of Old Peru* (Berlin, 1924): 106

Lothrop, S. K., *Tulum, an Archaeological Study of the East Coast of Yucatan*, Carnegie Institution of Washington, Pub. 335 (Washington, D.C., 1924): 91

Marquina, Ignacio, *Arquitectura prehíspánica*, Memorias del Instituto Nacional de Antropología e Historia, I (Mexico, 1951): 8, 10, 13, 15, 21, 29, 39, 60, 87, 88, 93, 95

Maudslay, A. P., *Biologia Centrali-Americana*, IV (London, 1896–99): 74, 77, 78, 79

Morley, Sylvanus G., *The Ancient Maya*, 3d ed., rev. by George W. Brainerd (Stanford University, 1956): 58, 96

National Geographic Society, Washington, D.C.: 112

Peabody Museum, Harvard University, Cambridge, Mass.: 11, 64, 68, 70, 92, 98

Pinney, Roy, Photo Library, Inc., New York: 113

Proskouriakoff, Tatiana, *An Album of Maya Architecture*, Carnegie Institution of Washington, Pub. 558 (Washington, D.C., 1946): 57, 69, 81

Revista mexicana de estudios antropológicos, VIII, 1946: 12

Silverstone, Marilyn, Nancy Palmer Photo Agency, New York: 101

Stephens, John L., *Incidents of Travel in Central America, Chiapas and Yucatan*, Harper and Brothers (New York, 1841): 72, 76

Squier, Ephraim G., *Peru Illustrated* (New York, 1879): 104, 120, 122

University Museum, Philadelphia, Photographic Collections: 82, 84, 89, 90, 108, 109